For information, contact:
McConnell Publishing, Ltd.
P.O. Box 447
Black Earth, WI 53515
(608) 767-2435
www.patriciamcconnell.com

Cover design by Julie Mueller, jam graphics & design
Cover photo of Theo, by Kimberly M. Wang
Back cover photo of Pilot, by Sarah Babcock
Printed in the United States of America

9 8 7 6 5 4

CASEY

LOVE HAS NO AGE LIMIT

Welcoming an Adopted Dog into Your Home

Patricia B. McConnell, PhD
Karen B. London, PhD

TABLE OF CONTENTS

MEEKA

INTRODUCTION

Bugsy was in trouble when Karen first met him. Half Black Lab and half handsome stranger, he was a 60-pound, two-and-half year old who sometimes sat on cue but had no other training. More problematically, he barked at visitors, lunged at other dogs when on leash, chased cars, and would sometimes take off if he got loose outside. After Karen adopted him, patience and consistent training allowed him to progress so much that he became her demo dog in training classes, assisted her in treating dogs who were reactive to other dogs and took long, off-leash walks in the country.

Bo Peep was going to be put down. A young Great Pyrenees, she was born with structural problems and couldn't stand up on her hind legs. She dragged herself forward by her forelegs, pushing the straw on the barn floor behind her like a seal through water. That's when Patricia took her in, wondering what in the world she was thinking. One year and three surgeries later, Bo Peep was a healthy and happy sweetheart of a dog who was loved by people, other dogs and the sheep she gently guarded for the next nine years.

Most stories about the adoption of adolescent or adult dogs aren't quite that dramatic, but still, there is something very special about bringing an older dog into your home. Puppies come with little experience behind them, acting like furry, little sponges who are primed to soak up knowledge. They attach themselves to any one who will feed them and rub their bellies, and then follow them everywhere. Older dogs ("older" as in "not-a-puppy-anymore") are different in some ways; they arrive with a history behind them, having learned what to expect from life as they matured. They may come ready to bond with you the moment they enter your house, or they may need a little time to get to know you. They may come with good habits or bad ones. Some dogs will come and ease themselves into your life within twenty-four hours, while others, like Bugsy and Bo Peep, may require a lot more time, knowledge and patience.

Adopting a dog who needs a new home is a wonderful thing, but right now there isn't much written about bringing home a mature dog, and how to forge a relationship with something other than a puppy. We want to help you start this adventure off on the right paw, walking side-by-side with a dog we hope will soon become one of your best friends.

We know there are many questions that arise when you welcome a new dog into your home. (We've often asked ourselves these questions, including, "Oh, dear, what have I gotten myself into?), but we also suspect that you might be too busy to read a lengthy book. *Love Has No Age Limit* covers the most common and important issues that you might encounter, based on our own experiences and input from other trainers and behaviorists as well as shelter and rescue experts. We can't both keep it concise and provide detailed explanations of every question that might arise, but included is what you most need to know during the first month after you adopt a new dog. At the end of the booklet we've added a list of resources if you need more information on a specific issue.

When you get a new dog, it's natural to want to know everything at once, but don't worry about reading this booklet straight through. If you don't have your dog yet, we recommend reading the Preparation section first. If you are standing in the living room with your new dog thinking "Now what?," your first stop should be the Coming Home and Settling In sections. Otherwise, go to the section that you need right now and read the rest when you get a chance. Most of all, please accept best wishes and crossed paws from us, and the spirits of our own rescued dogs, for a wonderful life with the newest member of your family.

PILOT

PREPARATION

Sometimes a new dog comes into your life unexpectedly, and the best you can do is create a mental "to do" list as you drive home with a bundle of fur in your car. But if you have the chance, preparing for your dog's arrival is time well spent. Being prepared makes the transition smoother and allows you to focus on your new friend rather than on rearranging the house or buying supplies. However, we've both taken dogs home with little advance warning to either foster, adopt, or even just to dog sit, and it's worked out just fine. So, don't panic if you're driving home with a dog unexpectedly—you're not alone. But if you have the luxury of advance notice, here are some things to consider:

Supplies. What most people need for their dogs is simple: a 4 to 6 foot leash (no retractable leashes at first please), a comfortable basic flat collar and an ID tag with your phone number on it, food and water bowls (though you can use anything from your kitchen at first), dog food and a crate or small pen. We'd also add in a few chew toys, especially a hollow one like a Kong® that can be stuffed with food, and a variety of treats. These are the basics, and once you have them, the next step is to consider what other items might be good to have around.

Toys are wonderful things, but don't spend a fortune on them right away; wait until you know what your dog likes best. Buy a few toys that represent the most common kinds (perhaps a ball, a plush toy and a squeaky toy) and watch to see which ones, if any, your dog likes best.

If you want your dog to use a crate, you might as well pick one up now. You might not be able to make use of it the first night, but it's still great to have right away so that you can begin to familiarize your dog with it. Similarly, pens, gates, and fences may make life easier, depending on the dog and the layout of your home and yard. Rounding out the list of useful dog items are a dog bed, grooming supplies, poop bags, and an enzymatic cleaner for cleaning up after accidents and preventing them in the future.

Dog-Proofing. Think of "dog-proofing" your house as an insurance policy. Your dog will be safer if you've prevented access to potential hazards, and your house will be safer if you protect it from your dog's powerful jaws. Besides, it's harder to bond with a dog who has just eaten your firstborn's baby book or lifted his leg on the family's heirloom quilt. (Though it's still possible, and we have heard the tales to prove it. Consider these traumas to be material for great stories in the future.)

Decide right away what rooms will be accessible to your new dog. It's smart to start by making only part of the house available, and then to expand that area as you become confident about your dog's bathroom and chewing habits. Perhaps you have a room that is clearly less dog friendly than the rest of the house because it houses an expensive crystal collection, or is full of electronic equipment, and therefore lots of electrical cords. Or perhaps you have a rarely used room that just begs to be snuck into and anointed with urine. Whatever the reason, we recommend that you restrict your dog's access to an area that allows you to keep an eye on her until you know her better. Think of "house privileges" as something that should be earned.

Dog-proofing a home is usually a continuous process that varies with each dog, depending on personality and experience. In the beginning, prioritize your efforts by keeping your dog safe from dangers such as electrical cords, dangerous cleaning supplies, household chemicals, sugar free gum with xylitol (which can be fatal to dogs) and potentially toxic plants, like lilies and philodendrons. Put irreplaceable items, such as photo albums or a toy that a child uses as a security blanket out of reach. If you have other pets, think about where each should be when the new dog enters the house. Let caution be your guide; consider where you'll put the cat to avoid a surprise meeting, and how you'll handle introductions between dogs. (See *Coming Home: The First Day* for details about introductions to the other animals in your family.)

A substantial amount of dog-proofing a house consists of changing the habits of the people who live there, at least until you know more about what is tempting to your new dog. For example, it's a good idea to get used to removing food and tissue boxes from the coffee table or counter, making leather items such as jackets, shoes, and gloves inaccessible, storing kids' toys off the floor, and remembering to close the doors that block access to areas that, at least for now, are off limits to the dog.

Setting up the house. Rearranging the house is a time-honored part of preparing for the arrival of a new dog. If you have an opportunity to do that before your new dog arrives, here are some questions that will help you figure out how to accommodate your new family member:

• Where's the best place for a crate (if you plan to use one)? Generally dogs do best if their crates are in rooms that you frequently use, but that aren't in high traffic areas or in front of windows.

• Should we get her a dog bed? Lots of dogs love having their own beds. Place some comfy dog beds (some are quite inexpensive) by your bed and by the couch where you spend time in the evenings. You can encourage her to use it by putting chew toys in it.

• What's the best place for her food and water bowls? Find a spot where she can use them without blocking traffic into the kitchen or hallway.

• Where will you store her food and treats? Be sure not to leave them anywhere that allows her to chew her way into them (and then blame her!)

• Do you have a spot for a "toy box?" Toy boxes can be great fun for both of you ("Go get your toys!" or "Time to put your toys away!") besides helping to keep your living room floor from looking like the aftermath of a windstorm in a pet store.

• Where should I put the leash, treats and clean up bags? Decide ahead of time where you will store these items so that they are available when and where you need them. A hook or shelf by the back door is often a handy place to keep them.

• If you can, gate off the area that leads to the front door—the starting point of many an escaped dog and a panicked chase through the neighborhood.

House Rules. Have a family meeting and decide on the rules of the house. Will the dog be allowed on the couch or beds? (We suggest waiting on that for a few weeks; better to start off conservatively while you're getting to know your dog.) Is begging from the table going to be allowed? If not, be sure everyone in the family is on board. Most importantly, get consensus from the family about what is and is not going to be allowed or encouraged. Caution: Be sure that your "rules" don't create unreasonable expectations of a new dog. It's one thing to agree "no feeding from the table" and another to demand that an adopted dog "knows" not to jump up on visitors.

Do Your Homework. If you have the opportunity, find out all you can about your new dog. You may not have a chance to do this, and if that's the case, don't worry, but if you can, ask some questions. If he was in a shelter or foster home, what do we know about his earlier life? What does he love, respond to, or appear afraid of? The key here is to ask specific questions, avoiding generic ones that provide little information. For example, say your new dog was in a foster home with three other dogs. Rather than asking

"How is he with other dogs?" ask, "What would he do if he was eating his dinner and another dog came over toward him?" Or, "Did he ever growl at another dog, and if so, what was happening when he did?" Be clear that you're not asking for a judgment—maybe he growled at another dog because that other dog is a bully—but rather to get information. Of course, how he behaves in one environment isn't always predictive of how he'll behave at your house, but it is still valuable to learn as much as you can.

Bring Home Some Comfort. This is another tip that you may or may not be able to follow, and no worries if you can't. If possible, bring home a towel or blanket that your adopted dog has slept on to make him feel more comfortable when he settles in to his new home. Familiar sights tend to make people feel more relaxed, but familiar smells are more comforting to dogs. It's also a good idea to bring home a few days worth of the food he had been eating to help keep his tummy from getting upset.

Should We Have a Welcome Home Party? Nope! Keep the number of visits from friends to a minimum for a few days, and have only one or two people come over at a time. That way you'll avoid overwhelming her while giving yourself a chance to learn more about her. Is she comfortable with all visitors? A tad nervous around unfamiliar men or children? In the beginning she'll have enough new things to deal with, so go slow in the beginning, and ask the family with five children to wait awhile.

BERNIE

COMING HOME: THE FIRST DAY

The Car Ride Home. If you have the opportunity, think through the ride home before you pick up your dog. Your first decision is where to put the dog on the way home. A crate is the safest way to transport a dog, if one will fit in your car and if the dog will tolerate it. If a crate isn't an option, at least put her in the safest spot, which is in the back of the car rather than in the front seat.

Ideally, have at least two people bring the dog home, one who can drive, and the other who can attend to the dog. Bring along some tasty treats to try luring the dog into the car. Many dogs may not be food motivated if they are stressed by the newness of the situation, but it's worth giving it a try. Have the person who has been taking care of the dog put her into the car if that becomes necessary—it's always better to have a familiar person do the lifting to avoid scaring the dog or eliciting a defensive snap or nip.

We hope you won't need them, but it's better to be safe than sorry, so bring some old towels to clean up messes. It's no fun to hear a dog lose his lunch in your car when you have a long drive ahead of you and nothing to clean it up with.

Our last bit of advice about the car ride home is simple, but it requires planning and commitment: Go directly home—don't stop for any errands, no matter how quick!

What To Do First? You're home, now what? Before you do anything else, take your dog outside on leash right away and let her sniff around. Even if you have a securely fenced yard, we suggest keeping her on leash, making sure it's attached *before* you let her out of the car. "Secure" fences often aren't as secure as you think, and if you have a slightly shy dog she may be hard to call back to you or to bring into the house. Please take this caution about keeping a new dog on leash seriously; an escaped dog is one of the most common problems that people experience with adopted dogs. Remember, almost all young puppies will automatically stay close to you, but most dogs over the age of five or six months are going to be far more independent. You can avoid a lot of stress and heartbreak by remembering this important difference between puppies and older dogs.

House Training 101: Besides making friends, house training is "job one" right now. The first few hours and days can make all the difference between this going smoothly or turning into a problem. For now, act as though you just brought home a puppy who has no idea where the bathroom is, because in a sense, you did. Grown dogs may be potty trained in one house, but not in another. Make no assumptions, no matter what anyone has told you, and start off right away teaching your dog the location of the bathroom.

If you're reading this before you've brought her into the house, take your dog outside where you want her to potty and walk around with her. She may not go—often dogs who are feeling a tad anxious won't—but that's okay, you gave it a try and can take her out again soon. Once inside, don't let her run around the house by herself. Take a page from puppy training books, and ensure that she is always either 1) in clear view inside, 2) in a crate or other small area or 3) outside with you. That way you'll avoid a quick "mistake" that can lead to a bad habit of sneaking away and relieving herself in the guest room. Things usually go best if you introduce her to just a few rooms at a time. Close off the little-used guest room or basement, and keep her in the rooms where you spend the most time. Gradually allow her access to other areas of the house, but only when you are confident she has learned to potty outside.

Take her out often, at least every thirty minutes or so, and don't wait for her to "tell" you she has to go potty. It's your job to get her outside to the right place, don't leave the burden on her shoulders. Besides, she might have been telling you in dog language for 20 minutes, but you think she's coming up to get petted. (If dogs could write books, they'd put this in bold, capital letters.) If you take her out and she doesn't go, be prepared for her to trot inside and want to go on the living room carpet. Frustrating though it may be, this is extremely common. Just develop the habit of watching her carefully, taking her out long before she needs to go, and being patient when you take her outside.

When she does potty outside, be ready to reinforce her with great treats. Keep some handy beside the door that you can grab on the way out, or in your pocket so that you can give her a treat immediately after she eliminates. Don't wait to give her a cookie when you're heading back inside together— that's reinforcing her for leaving the yard, not going potty in it. You're better off casually following her around, saying "good!" as soon as she finishes, and immediately giving her a treat. Some dogs are resistant to eliminating when they are on the leash, so be patient and persistent. We like to put eliminating outside on cue. ("Get Busy" is a common cue, though "Hurry Up" is appropriate during winter in northern climates!) Establishing a cue will help you later on when you're late for work and you need to get her out one more time before you leave.

Oops, Somebody Had An Accident: If (when?) you catch her having an accident in the house, don't yell or rub her nose in it. That will at best confuse her, and more likely alarm her so that the lesson she learns is either "Never urinate or defecate in front of a person," or "I need to be careful. This person is a little crazy." Take this advice seriously; we've known a multitude of dogs who would hold off urinating outside while beside their owners, wait until they could get back into the house and find some privacy, and relieve themselves on the bedroom carpet. If you see her start to go in the house, distract her with hand claps or "Uh Oh!" and immediately take her outside, giving lots of praise and treats for going outside. If you find a puddle or pile after the fact, say nothing to her, roll up a newspaper, and hit yourself on the head with it for not taking her out earlier. Put her in another room, clean it up with a good enzymatic cleaner designed for the purpose (avoid strong household cleaners because they can set the stain or the smell permanently), and ponder what you might be able to do to prevent it from happening again.

Introducing Your Dog to the House. When you first enter the house with your new dog, hopefully after she's eliminated, stay calm and relaxed to model the appropriate mood for your dog. Stay close by while you are giving your dog a tour. Keep it casual and relaxed, giving her a chance to sniff around. Ideally, there should be nothing lying around that you'd rather she leave alone. If she starts to chew on something that is off limits such as the carpet or the furniture, distract her and give her something appropriate to chew on. Show her where she'll be sleeping and get out a toy or chew bone to help her learn that this is her spot. (We'll talk about sleeping arrangements later.)

After the initial tour to give her the lay of the land, plan on some quiet time. Settle into your favorite spot, maybe even on the floor, and encourage her to come cozy in with you. If she's not shy or fearful, this is a great time to teach her the joys of belly rubs. If she seems to enjoy it, keep up the petting, but don't force it. If she's pacing nervously or clearly is not yet comfortable, consider another visit outdoors or provide her with something to chew on to keep her occupied. Don't give her a chew toy if there are other dogs in the house until you know more about how the dogs will interact. Exactly how to handle these first few hours is difficult to prescribe in detail, because your behavior should be driven by your dog's responses to you and your home. What's most important is to be observant, not to push things, and to take her outside far more often than you think you need to in order to jump start the house training process. Don't worry if she seems a bit anxious and unsettled. That's common for the first few days, and often goes away once the environment starts to become familiar.

Introductions to the Human Family. The main goal of each introduction is for it be a positive experience for the dog. That is most likely achieved if everyone is calm and low key so that the new dog is not overwhelmed. This is especially important if the dog is a bit cautious, and if there are children in the house. As we all know, children can often be, uh . . . a bit enthusiastic, and in their well-intentioned eagerness to love the dog, they can end up being frightening rather than welcoming. Specifically, kids (and adults, too, for that matter) should refrain from picking up the dog, hugging and kissing the dog, patting the top of the dog's head, or engaging in staring contests. All of these actions are ones that many kids will be inclined to do, but that almost all dogs dislike.

To prevent cornering or overwhelming the dog, have family members meet the dog one at a time. Each person should try to make a good impression in two ways: First, they should be calm, patient, and approachable. That means they should be standing or squatting quietly, turned a little bit to the side, and should wait to let the dog approach them. Everyone should talk in a calm voice without getting overly loud or excited, and should avoid leaning and looming over the dog. Pats on the head as well as hugs and kisses should be avoided, since most dogs find them annoying or frightening in the same way that children object to being pinched on the cheeks by aging relatives. If the dog approaches, scratching or petting the chest is a much better option. If the dog shies way, hold off on any attempts to make physical contact, at least for now. The second way to make a good impression is to have everyone offer the dog something that will make her happy, such as extra yummy dog treats, like a piece of chicken or liver. ("Mmmm, good things come from you! I like you!")

Introductions to the Canine Family. There's no single plan for dog-dog introductions that works best for every dog. A detailed description of all the situations we can think of would require its own book. However, there are some general guidelines that can increase the likelihood of it being a positive experience for everyone.

• If you have more than one other dog, have your new one meet the residents one at a time.

• Conduct the initial meeting outside rather than inside, and in a quiet, open area such that the dogs are not forced to interact in a small space. There are advantages to having the dogs meet off territory, but if that is not possible, the backyard is far better than inside the house. Outside is always better: If you allow the dogs to meet outside they have the opportunity to urinate and therefore "meet" each other through the scent of their urine, rather than being forced to investigate each other at close range.

• Dogs get tense around gates, doorways, and other thresholds, so avoid introductions in these areas. Conduct the introductions in the middle of an open area to avoid letting tension develop because space constraints have forced the dogs to be too close together before they are ready.

• If it is safe to do so (i.e. the area is securely fenced and both dogs have a history of being good with other dogs), have both dogs meet with their leashes dropped to the ground. If that is not possible, keep the leashes loose at all times. Long lines (thin, light leashes that are 10 or 12 feet long) make this easier, but with steady effort and attention this is possible even with 6-foot leashes.

• At the start of the meeting, keep moving. If possible, have two adults (humans!) out with the dogs, and use your actions to influence the dog's behavior. If the people move forward in a purposeful way, the dogs often follow them, which avoids tense greetings in which dogs are forced to get acquainted in close contact.

• Don't hover. If there is any tension at all, boxing in the dogs or making them feel confined will only make things worse. Keep them away from fences and walls if possible, and don't lean over any of the dogs.

• If the dogs seem tense with each other, you should move away from them, rather than towards them. We sympathize—this is counter to what is natural, so prepare ahead of time by reminding yourself that it is the right course of action. Moving away diffuses tension while moving closer adds to it. Say, "this way" in a light, happy voice, clap your hands together to get their attention, and stride away.

• Do all that you can to keep your own body relaxed. If you're nervous, your dog might pick up on it and become nervous himself. Try to breathe normally, stay loose, move around, and avoid staring. Make your own manner light and breezy to set the right tone for the dogs.

• To eliminate any issues with possessiveness or sharing, make the initial meeting a food-free, toy-free zone.

• If you have any reason to suspect that meeting another dog will be a challenge, based on your knowledge of either dog's history or behavior, have a qualified behaviorist or trainer advise you and help monitor the initial interactions.

• Once the dogs have met outside and are going to be together inside, bring the *new dog inside first*, and the resident dog in second. If the resident dog is at all territorial, this tends to diffuse some of that "Who's that entering my house!?" tension.

Helping Dogs to Get Along. After the dogs have met each other, the obvious question is "Now what?" The answer, of course, depends on the individual dogs and how they are doing together. Many dogs have an easy relationship from the time of the initial introduction, and if you're lucky, that will be the case with your dogs. However, it's always wise to proceed cautiously when integrating a new dog into a home that includes at least one other dog. Here are some suggestions to help the relationship get off on the right paw:

• Give the dogs enough space to get away from each other, along with opportunities to be alone and away from each other entirely. This kind of "down time" does wonders for helping them enjoy the time they DO spend together. It's especially important to give geriatric dogs time alone to recover from all the excitement and change.

• Until you know them much better, don't leave them loose together when you leave the house; keep them in separate rooms or in their own crates.

• If your new dog is comfortable taking walks in the neighborhood, take the dogs on lots of leash walks together. Walking side-by-side, investigating interesting smells, is the way two dogs would naturally form a relationship, so do what you can to help them "be dogs" together by taking them on excursions. If one dog is a bit nervous around the other, have two people take one dog each on a side-by-side walk, keeping several feet between them and letting the dogs explore the neighborhood without being in physical contact.

• When you are home, continue to watch the dogs, paying attention to how they react to each other and behave in one another's presence. What's most important is to avoid forcing an interaction, and to be on the look out for any signs of tension. We elaborate on this in the *Behavior Problems Between Dogs in the House* section, but in general, watch for growls or snaps, stiffening of the body, and hard stares from one dog to another. If these signs of tension occur, try distracting the dogs with smooches or claps, and redirect their attention to you. If it continues after a few days, you'd be wise to give the shelter, the foster family, a professional trainer or behaviorist a call.

Meeting Cats. If you have one or more cats, be thoughtful about how you introduce your new dog to the household's felines. Some cats are dog savvy and have little trouble dealing with them unless the dog is truly aggressive. These types of cats will stand their ground if the dog bothers them, hissing or using their paws to bat at a dog who doesn't get the message to leave it alone. Other cats will try to run away, and that can be great fun for the dog, but not so much fun for the cat. A small number of dogs are truly aggressive to cats, even if they don't have "Cat Killer" on their rap sheets. That's why we encourage you to put safety first, and use leashes or secure gates to prevent contact between a new dog and your cat until you are confident the dog isn't going to cause any harm.

In order to prevent trouble, especially with the cats in the "running away" category, keep these things in mind: 1) Do not give a new dog a chance to chase the cat. Period. It could result in serious injuries, and even if they aren't hurt, cats can be traumatized and take many weeks to recover. 2) Cat chasing is a lot easier to prevent than it is to stop—even one wild-eyed chase that's more fun than your dog has ever had in his entire life will be hard to counteract, so pull out all the stops to prevent chasing. 3) Once you are comfortable letting them be together, the cat still needs escape options, whether it's a gate the dog can't jump over (but the cat can), into a crate too small for the dog, or, best of all, onto something too high for the dog to reach. Vertical escape options include cat trees, high windowsills, or tall, sturdy furniture. Ideally, the cat has a place in every room to get away from the dog if the dog and the cat are allowed to be together. In addition, be sure that the cat has easy access to food, water and her litter box without running the gauntlet past your dog(s).

Be proactive about preventing trouble. Whenever you can't monitor them closely, separate the dog and cat by putting them in different sections of the house. Brief encounters that go well are a great start to their relationship and it's better to quit while you're ahead. In many cases, one or two sessions are all you need and your cat and dog will be cuddled up on the couch in no time. In other families, things may proceed much more slowly. Keep in mind that if your cat has never had a dog in the house she might be very frightened, even hiding under the bed or in a closet just because she can hear the dog. If that describes your cat, let her gain confidence at her own pace, never forcing her into an interaction that scares her. It can take scaredy cats up to six months to warm up to a four-legged newcomer, so put on your patience hat and be sure that your cat has access to the essentials, including lots of love and affection from you.

If you do see signs of serious trouble between your animals—your cat is so frightened she's stopped eating, or the dog appears to be stalking the cat—you'd be wise to seek help from a behaviorist who can come in and evaluate the situation. Just remember that cats are much slower to adjust to new social situations than dogs and they never, ever want to be trapped or forced into anything.

Stay Close to Home. Although exercise is a good thing, in the beginning you might not know enough about your dog to predict how she'll respond while on a neighborhood walk. For at least the first few days, spend most of your outdoor time close to home so that you can gather information about how your dog will respond to environmental distractions—from a neighbor's loose dog to children playing on the sidewalk or to a noisy truck roaring by. You want to be sure that your dog has some good experiences in her new home before you venture out much, so take her into the front yard for brief periods and stay close to the house until she looks curious and comfortable. First impressions matter as much to dogs as to people, so if you can't guarantee that they'll be good, plan to avoid situations in which you have no control over what your dog is going to encounter.

Dogs Don't Enjoy a Day at the Spa. Unless your dog arrives in a desperate condition (filthy, matted or covered in fleas and ticks), try to avoid giving her a bath until she's settled in a bit. Although most dogs can get used to baths and even willingly jump into the tub for a quick shower, few dogs really enjoy it, and some are downright terrified. Finding out how much your dog hates a bath is probably not the best way to begin your relationship, so avoid giving her a bath, trimming her nails or doing any grooming until things have calmed down a bit. If you absolutely have to bathe your dog, use lots of treats to make it as enjoyable as possible. Some dogs will refuse food, being too nervous to eat, but others will be happy that although they hated the bath, at least it came along with chicken!

LUCY

SETTLING IN: ESTABLISHING DAILY ROUTINES

Where's the Bedroom? If at all possible, let your new friend sleep in the same room as you. Dogs are social animals and sleeping all alone in a strange place is tough for some dogs. If that's not an option, settle your dog down in an area of the house where you and your dog will spend time during the day. If you were fortunate enough to obtain one, put down the towel you brought from his former home to surround him with familiar smells.

What's most important about your dog's new bedroom is that: 1) Your new dog is safe—no toxic chemicals in easily opened cabinets, no screen doors to the great outdoors that can too easily be opened, 2) The area is dog-proofed. Accidents should be easy to clean up, there are no priceless antiques in the area and a little bit of chewing is not going to be a crisis, and 3) The location is cozy and quiet, with plenty of scents that say "we live here!" Remember how important scent is to dogs; the stronger the scent of his new family— you, other dogs (if relevant), and other people—the more likely it is that your new dog will feel comfortable. Asking your new dog to sleep in the basement or garage, where you never go except to do the laundry, is tough on a social animal. If you have other dogs, by all means try to set it up so that they can safely sleep in the same area, either with some crates (at least for the new dog) or separated by gates.

To Crate or Not to Crate? Crates are an excellent choice to prevent house soiling and destructive chewing, but dogs have never read the chapter that says they are "den animals." That's because they aren't. (Well, okay, they can't read either.) "Wild" dogs go into dens to deliver their puppies in safety, but otherwise they choose to sleep out in the open. However, dogs can be taught to enjoy their crates, relating to them as safe and peaceful places to relax. If your dog arrives crate trained, count your blessings and continue the positive association by placing the crate in a quiet, but not isolated, place. Ask the dog to "crate up" and put a hollow toy stuffed with food in the crate to sweeten the pot.

Meanwhile, if she's never been in a crate, set one up in a quiet but familiar area and toss treats inside for her to enjoy. Don't even think about shutting the door at first; let her poke her head inside and then eat the treat and back out. If she's too hesitant even to poke her head inside, start by putting treats just outside the crate door and let her eat those. Repeat this over the next few days, gradually tossing the treat farther back inside the crate. Once she'll charge into the crate as if she owns it, try shutting the door, tossing more treats inside and opening it before she's done eating them. Gradually leave the door shut for increasing periods of time, giving her a hollow toy stuffed with food for entertainment.

At least half the time, open the door and take out the toy before she is done with it (as long as she has not shown any signs of aggression over food or objects). When you open the door she'll think, "Wait! I'm not ready to come out!" Perfect—that's the reaction you want! Your just using reverse psychology, and it can work as well on dogs as it does on people. Your goal is to teach her that good things happen when she's in the crate, and that the door will open before she knows it. If you try this and she growls at you, then drop it from your repertoire and read the *Resource Guarding* section.

If she barks or whines for a few minutes, wait for her to be quiet before you let her out. You don't want her to learn that vocalizing gets you to come running. If she won't settle down in a crate and you have to leave her, you can try gating her into an area in which she can do little harm. Small dogs often do well in exercise pens (also called ex pens), which are portable pens that allow small dogs more movement than crates, but aren't sufficient to confine large dogs who could either knock them down or jump over them. If your goal is to be able to use a crate with her eventually, see the *Resources* section for more information about crate training.

Another option for nighttime is having her sleep on the floor in a doggy bed beside your own. In this case, either close the bedroom door or attach the dog with a leash to something big and solid. If using a leash, do so carefully, such that the dog can't leap over something and be hung up by the leash itself. In some cases, you might welcome the dog into your bed right away, but note our cautions about taking things slowly.

I'm hungry. The way to a dog's heart is often through his stomach, so make some early decisions about when, what, and where you are going to feed your new dog.

When to Feed: It's best to give your dog two meals a day, rather than one large one, but plenty of dogs have thrived on the latter, so don't think of it as a deal breaker. Structured routines are good for dogs who have experienced a lot of change in their lives (or none at all), but most dogs don't need you to be a slave to the clock. It won't hurt to feed a dog at 6:00 instead of 5:00 if you get stuck at work, but do try to be relatively consistent. A few dogs do well, or even better, with food left out free choice, but in general it is best to feed meals yourself. That way you can monitor intake, create predictable bathroom habits, provide fresh, healthy food and remind your dog that the goodies come from you.

What to Feed: How long do you have? Even a brief discussion about what to feed your dog could fill up an entire book, so we'll stick to essentials: First, on day one and day two, try to feed your new dog what she was eating before you adopted her. Over the next week or two, mix the old food with what you've selected to allow her tummy to adjust. Second, if you plan to feed your dog a commercial food, read the ingredients on the labels and choose ones that list real meat first ("chicken" versus "chicken meal"). Be careful about meaningless labels like "all natural." Apologize to the marketing team that spent weeks coming up with cool names and lovable labels, and base your decisions on what is actually inside the can or bag. Third, once you're sure her stomach has settled, don't hesitate to add small amounts of freshly cooked vegetables like broccoli, string beans, parsley, and squash to her dinner; just keep your additions to no more than ten to twenty percent of the food. Introduce new foods gradually and do not feed troublesome foods like onions, raisins and chocolate, which are dangerous for dogs. Fourth, save some of her dinner as training treats, so that you can use food as a reinforcement without making her fat. If you'd like to learn more about good commercial foods, or cooking for your dog yourself, a great resource is *The Whole Dog Journal* (www.whole-dog-journal.com).

Where to Feed: If this is your only dog and you have no children, it's probably most convenient to feed your dog in the kitchen. Pick a place that is not in the path where everybody walks—no dog can relax if she knows someone is about to barge into the room and bump into her while she's eating. If you have other dogs or youngsters who might not know to leave a dog alone when she's eating, feed your dog in her crate or in an area where she is safe from others, and where others are safe from her if she feels a need to defend her food. Remember you might not have any idea what happened to her around mealtime, and you have no idea yet what she will do around food once she settles into your household.

We don't want to belabor this, or make you nervous around your new dog, but please make no assumptions about how she'll behave around food when you get her home. She may have passed a "resource guarding" test at the shelter, but just like people, dogs behave differently in different environments, so be cautious in the beginning. If you do see signs of trouble, read the section on resource guarding and contact the shelter, rescue group, a well-qualified local trainer or behaviorist for assistance.

Be Thoughtful About Neighborhood Walks. Although most dogs love to go on walks, not all dogs should go on a stroll around the neighborhood when you first adopt them. Even a quiet suburb can be overwhelming to a dog who has had little socialization or exposure to the world when younger. After a day or two, if your dog seems relaxed and comfortable, take her out for a short walk of 5-10 minutes. Choose the quietest walk possible, avoiding places where your dog might become scared by machinery, barking dogs, or screaming children. Don't feel bad if your dog does not seem ready for a walk yet. Remember, the goal is to provide your dog with exercise and stimulation, and a walk isn't the only way to do that. You can take her out to potty, and spend lots of time in quiet places, perhaps teaching her tricks and how to play with toys, until she is more comfortable being out and about.

On the other hand, neighborhood walks taken together can be a great way for a new dog to become comfortable with a resident dog, as long as your new dog is comfortable in the great outdoors. This is not the time, however, for your adopted dog to be greeting other dogs in the neighborhood, so walk across the street if you see other dogs coming, and avoid "high traffic" times until you get to know your dog better.

The House is Not a Chew Toy. Just as with house training, make no assumptions about how your new dog will behave when you are not watching her like a hawk. Treat her as if she is a puppy, and assume that she'll chew on your slippers if you leave them on the living room floor. Dog proof your house until you get a better sense of how mouthy your dog is going to be. Of course, a typical one-year old Lab mix is going to behave a lot differently than a twelve-year old Greyhound, being much more likely to chew on, well, anything, but you'd be wise to be cautious for the first week or so at least, no matter what you expect her behavior will be.

Provide lots of safe chew toys, keep your own belongings off the low tables and floors, and keep her in the same room as you so that you can keep an eye on her. If she does pick up something she shouldn't have, avoid charging at her, raising your voice or provoking her into a "catch me if you can!" game. Many dogs love chase games, and will start going out of their way to find things to steal to get you going. Other dogs may react with fear or an attempt to guard items from you. Instead, try to distract her and redirect her to something appropriate. While she's settling in, don't make too big a fuss over objects that aren't valuable or can't harm her. Just make a mental note to do a better job of keeping the house picked up, and teaching her what objects are appropriate chew toys.

Home Alone? Some dogs in rescue organizations and shelters have grown up surrounded by other dogs, possibly hundreds of them if they are from a puppy mill or a racing background. Even dogs who have been "crate trained" may have never been left alone in a house. No matter what the background of your new dog, teach her that when you leave, you'll come right back. If she's crate trained, put her in a crate with a treat, leave the house with your keys and coat, and come back in *three seconds* (yes, we said seconds, not minutes) to demonstrate to her you'll return. Try that again a few times within a few days of bringing her home, leaving her for slightly longer periods. If she's not comfortable in a crate, try an ex pen or a gated room in which she can't hurt herself or destroy anything important.

We advise you not to leave a new dog loose in the house until you know her well. You simply don't know what is going to happen, and it's better to be safe than sorry. After she's been with you a few months, try leaving her loose in the house during short departures to test her out, gradually increasing the amount of time that she is home alone. Do NOT, under any circumstances, correct her if you come home and find she's gotten herself into trouble.

That "guilty" look is her attempt to keep you from getting angry at you, not a sign that she "knows" better. Quietly pick up the mess, and resolve to go backward a few steps.

We also don't advise leaving a new dog loose in the house with other dogs when you are gone for the first few months. We don't want to get a call from you about a serious and expensive medical emergency, so go slow until you have more information about how the dogs are going to do together.

If your dog panics when left alone or seems anxious when you are about to leave, go right to the section on Separation Anxiety, and take heart. Even anxious dogs can be taught to be comfortable when left alone, although it does take some time and attention.

Promote Good Behavior. Decide, if you haven't already, how you define "good behavior" and do all you can to help your new dog meet your expectations. Right now it's your job to avoid behavioral problems through management (for example, close doors, pick up shoes, remove food from the table promptly), and to distract her if she begins to do something wrong. For example, if your new Cattle Dog cross begins chomping on the couch (which you see right away because you're not leaving her alone to get into trouble, right?), distract her by clapping or making an abrupt noise, and immediately give her an appropriate chew toy. Of course, it's even better to be proactive by teaching her what you DO want her to do (give her a toy stuffed with food before she starts to chew up the couch), but nobody's perfect, and reacting quickly to an "oops" moment is the next best thing. See the *Training* section for more ideas about helping your dog learn what you want her to do.

TAMMY and SLIM JIM

GETTING TO KNOW EACH OTHER: BUILDING A RELATIONSHIP

Patience, Patience, Patience. When we asked people with experience in rescue what they think new owners need to know, the most common response by far was "to be patient." You may be prepared to enter into a close and emotional relationship with your new dog the day you bring her home, and you probably have expectations of who she should be, but your adopted dog has no such mind set. After all, you probably spent a long time thinking about adopting, while your new dog had no idea what to expect when you picked her up. Everything, including you, is new to her. Think of how you'd feel in an unfamiliar place surrounded by strangers; if you're like most people, you'd need some time to get comfortable. We don't mention the importance of patience lightly. In a recent survey by Best Friends Animal Society that looked at nearly 900 ex-breeding dogs adopted from puppy mills, owners reported that being patient with their dogs was more important than any other skill or attitude in helping their dogs adjust to their new lives as pets[1].

No matter what their background, adult dogs are similar to adult people in that they often need time to form social relationships. That's one of the most important differences between grown-up dogs and young puppies.

1 "Therapeutic insights into treating ex-breeder puppy mill dogs." Talk by Frank McMillan, DVM, Interdisciplinary Forum for Applied Animal Behavior, February 18, 2011, New Orleans, Louisiana)

Young pups are inherently dependent on their elders, and with rare exceptions, will instantly bond to their new humans. But adult dogs vary tremendously; some will lick your hand, kiss your face and not want to leave your side within minutes of meeting you. Other dogs are like people involuntarily thrown into a blind date, and have no concept of how to relate to you until they get to know you better. That doesn't mean they won't become your best friends, it just means that the level of closeness you reach in the first few days or weeks might be different than if your dog were an eight-week old pup.

As well as needing time to get to know the people in the household, adult dogs need time to acclimate to everything else that is new to them. That means you need to be patient with your dog's behavior and level of training, in addition to being patient about the development of a close social relationship. Just as humans need time to adapt to being in a new place (most people don't sleep well in a new bed until the third or fourth night, for example), the sensory systems of dogs are overwhelmed by new sights, sounds and smells for at least a couple of days. That's why it's important in the first few days to balance giving your new dog attention with giving her time and space to become comfortable in a new home and with everything she's encountering in it. It's difficult to be specific about how to help our dogs adjust, because every dog is different, but here are some general guidelines:

Commit Time for the First Few Days. Do whatever you can to spend as much time as possible with your new dog in the first few days. It's only by spending time together that you can learn more about your dog's habits and personality, and doing it early on will make adjusting to life together smoother for both of you.

There are lots of strategies for maximizing the time together in those first few days. The biggest hurdle for most of us is our work schedule—not everyone can free up an entire week to be with their new dog, even if they'd dearly love to. (Feel free to tell your employer that we recommend you take time off, but don't be surprised if your boss is not convinced by our professional opinion.) If you work during the week and can't get time off, the best time to get a dog is a weekend, so that you can have at least two days together before heading back to work. If possible, and there are others also working in your family, try to coordinate work schedules with other members of the household so that collectively, your free time adds up to a few days or even a week.

Regardless of your work obligations, clear the rest of your schedule as much as possible. Don't go out in the evenings if you can avoid it, and catch up as much as possible on errands before the dog arrives. It's best not to take any trips in the first couple of weeks after adopting your dog because the additional upheaval in a new routine can be a setback to your dog's adjustment. Of course, we're saying what is ideal—and we all know that life happens when we least expect it. Do your best and don't fret if you end up with the dog on a busy night through no fault of your own, or if an unplanned business trip comes up and ruins your best-laid plans.

What is most important is to balance interacting with your dog with letting her rest. Travel and change can be tiring for both people and dogs, so engage in what your dog enjoys without overdoing it. Take her outside to potty often (remember that house training is job one!), do a little light-hearted training and some petting or massage if your dog responds well to it, but give her the chance to just sniff around her new world or simply hang out in it.

Don't Scare Your Dog! Avoid fear-inducing punishments (now and forever)—no swatting, yelling or throwing things. That doesn't mean you should let her get away with murder or treat her as if she were made out of fine china. But your priority right now is to create a comfortable environment of stability, ease and trust, so do all you can to prevent problems, and spend your energy helping her adjust to a new environment.

Punishments that scare your dog don't provide any information about *the right way* to behave and they undermine the trust that is the basis of any good relationship. This is especially important for a dog who has been under-socialized or frightened in the past, and has been taught that people can be dangerous. See the *Training* section for advice about how to teach your dog manners in a fun and effective way.

Give Your Dog Some Space. Recently Patricia and a friend were at a shelter meeting an adult dog. They were meeting Missy, a female of unknown origin and background, who was becoming overly reactive in the busy, noisy environment of a shelter. Rather than greeting them, Missy dashed to a ball on the ground and brought it over for them to throw. After a few tosses, the friend put his hands on either side of Missy's head and before anyone could stop him, bent his head to hers and kissed her on the nose. Eeeeps! Without realizing it, he had put himself in danger. Direct eye contact coupled with face-to-face intimacy is not friendly to dogs, it's frightening. Most family dogs are used to it and tolerate it, however, it is not a safe or polite way to behave around a dog you don't know. Missy had not yet greeted any of us, and the shelter had no information about how comfortable she was around strangers. Luckily, she didn't react aggressively, but many dogs would have, so kiss your human family for now, but not your new dog until you know her better.

Be respectful when you are getting to know a new dog. Keep your face away from the dog's face, don't hug or grab at the dog, and avoid letting young children interact without carefully watching for signs of discomfort from the dog. Don't throw the dog in with other dogs in hopes it will all work out. Avoid dog parks and crowded play areas in your neighborhood where kids and other dogs might scare your new friend. This is a good time to be cautious. Be careful and don't push your dog into dealing with too much too soon. Can we say "patience" again here without being irritating?

See the Dog, Not the Story. This is excellent advice from someone with a rescue dog.[2] What your new dog needs most of all is the same thing a person needs—to be accepted and respected for who they are, to be "heard" and understood, rather than to be labeled. You may have been told a number of stories about your dog's history, but although it can be valuable to gather information, it's also important not to label your dog for the rest of his life as, for example, "abused" or "neglected." Your goal, beyond providing your new dog a safe and stable environment, is to honor him by letting him tell you who he is right now, accepting that, and acting accordingly. Just as you are no longer that little girl or boy who got bullied on the playground, your dog will grow and change as time goes on. Do all you can to see him for who he is NOW, not who he was years ago or who you think he should be.

Learn to "Read Your Dog." The more adept you are at translating the postures and expressions of your dog, the more you'll get to know her, and the better your relationship will be. Dogs and people share many emotional expressions, but we humans are often not very good at recognizing these facial changes once you include a black nose, a furry face and long ears. Additionally, some signals given by dogs are different than human ones, and that further adds to the confusion. Learn to be aware of stress-related signals like turning the head away, tongue flicking, closing the mouth while the body goes stiff and still, yawning when not sleepy, becoming frantically animated or obsessively sniffing the ground.

Here are some examples of the value of being able to "read" your dog: Imagine that you reach to pet your dog, and his reaction is to turn his head away, close his mouth and go still. These actions are signals that he's uncomfortable and doesn't want to be touched at the moment. In this case, you should withdraw your hand and give him some space. Or perhaps you ask your dog to lie down and he flicks out his tongue and yawns. He's not

2 Thank you Judi for your comment on Patricia's blog (www.theotherendoftheleash.com) on October 6, 2010.)

sticking out his tongue to be cute, and he may not be sleepy. Rather, his reaction—exhibiting two behaviors that often indicate low-level stress or anxiety—might be a sign that in his previous home, "lie down" meant something bad was about to happen. This would be a good time to teach him a different word for the same action, and link it with yummy treats.

Learning to understand another individual, especially one who belongs to another species, takes time and knowledge. Ideally, some time in the future you can enjoy some of the many great resources available on reading dogs (see the *Resources* section for ideas). For now, what is most important is being as observant as you can; much of "reading a dog" is simply focusing your attention on his face and posture and paying attention to what you see.

Who Are You Anyway? Because of the effect of a new environment, the true nature of your new dog may not appear right away. Truly traumatized dogs, or dogs raised in neglectful, sterile conditions, can take more than a year to come into their own, although most dogs show you their true colors sooner than that. However, even a well-adjusted adult dog can be a bit shell-shocked when you first bring him home, and the dog you have on day one might be very different than the dog you have in three days, three weeks, or three months. It is not uncommon for quiet dogs to become boisterous, dogs who are initially frantic to calm down, and for clingy dogs to become more independent.

Of course, both *genetics* and *past experiences* play important roles in influencing a dog's behavior. These two factors are what combine to create an adult dog's personality. Not surprisingly, inherently stable dogs from solid beginnings often adapt with ease to new surroundings, while dogs at the other end of the continuum—temperamentally nervous dogs with traumatic histories—will be much slower to adapt. It's often difficult to learn anything about your dog's genetics, but it might be possible to get information about his life before you got him.

If you are one of the lucky ones who knows the dog's former owners or at least people who have worked with or fostered the dog, ask what cues the dog responds to, what he loves, what makes him nervous, how he behaves around familiar and unfamiliar dogs, what his response is to people of all ages and both genders, how he reacts to cats, loud noises, and to being left alone. Ignorance is not bliss here; take advantage of any and all available information and use it to help smooth your new friend's transition from one life to another. However, don't worry if his past is a mystery and he arrives with no Owner's Manual attached to his collar—what's most important is to get to know who he is now, and how you can integrate him into your family.

He Won't Let Me Near Him! Some dogs might come to you profoundly damaged from being confined in a cage for many years, without any opportunity to interact, play or even move more than a few inches forward or backward. These poor dogs are often terrified of everything, of you and of any new sights, sounds or smells. Dogs who have been abused in this way are literally wired differently than normal dogs, and have no coping skills to deal with any kind of change. These dogs require tremendous patience and a lot of time before they begin to come out of their shells. If you have been so kind as to adopt a dog like this, what is most important is to give the dog a "safe house" which is a place where she can go and feel secure, and not have anything forced upon her. We'll talk more about how to help these kinds of dogs in the *Fearful Dogs* section.

Who Named This Dog Anyway? Don't like the name your dog came with? No problem, dogs can learn a new name as easily as you can. Just start by saying the new name and giving him something wonderful—whether it's a treat, a chin scratch or a play session—if he turns to look at you. Guard against using it for no reason or as a correction. You want him to love hearing his new name and turn happily toward you in anticipation when he hears it. He'll learn it within a few weeks at most, even faster if you link it consistently with something he likes.

BAILEY

VETERINARY CARE

Finding the Right Vet for You and Your Dog. To find a vet in your area who suits you and your dog, conduct a little research with friends and with the vets themselves. Some questions to ask include:

- Are they open to answering questions?
- Are they able to take time with you, or are they rushed with clients?
- Are they fairly traditional or do they have an interest in alternative medicine?
- Are they calm and gentle with animals?
- Do they consistently run on time?
- Do they have a specialty in their practice?

Get estimates of the charges and fees at several clinics so you can compare. Ask what they charge for vaccinations, annual check-ups, and common procedures such as spaying or neutering.

The First Visit. Unless your dog needs immediate medical care, give him a few weeks to settle in before you take him to the veterinary clinic. When you do go, make the first visit a positive experience, so that Fido leaves hoping he can come back soon. Request a "meet and greet" office visit and make it fun for your dog by asking everyone to give your dog yummy treats. Bring a variety of tasty snacks so that Fido gets special treats that make him extra happy. Leave your dog in the car if you can at first, so that you can quickly check that the lobby isn't full of seven dogs all barking at the same time. Once the coast is clear, bring him in and give him treats in both the lobby and an exam room, so that the entire clinic is just one, wonderful trick-or-treat experience.

You might try having your dog weighed, but don't push it if he resists. If he likes petting and massage, give him some of that loving, but only if you're sure he adores it. And even if he usually enjoys that sort of physical contact, don't interrupt his sniffing and exploring. If he is happily engaged, just let him be, keeping in mind that if he's having a good time, the visit is a success. Besides providing treats and attention, the people at the veterinarian's office don't need to do anything. The point of this visit is not medical care, but to provide a good experience so that future care is less stressful. If necessary, first call around to find a veterinary practice that is amenable to this kind of visit—it's not a bad way to evaluate how well they'll treat your dog in the future.

The Second Visit. Ideally, every visit to the vet will be a happy experience with treats and plenty of positive attention, but the purpose of the second visit should include a thorough check up. Such care usually includes investigating known medical issues, as well as getting some blood work done. Basic blood work allows vets to check for many health issues, and to serve as a baseline for comparison as your dog ages. Ask for a good guess on your dog's age and breeds if they are unknown, and leave with a good understanding of vaccination schedules, as well as safe and effective ways to control parasites.

Life Does Not Always Go According to Plan. Our advice about the first and second visits to the vet describes what we'd like to happen in a perfect world. Oh, you don't live in that world? Regrettably, neither do we. Starting with a cheerful, friendly visit to the vet where everything that happens to your dog is happy and fun—in other words, no medical examination or care whatsoever—is the best-case scenario. We understand that this may not always be possible or reasonable. If your new dog is dealing with matted fur, fleas and ticks, or needs to be examined so the vet can make a diagnosis, waiting to deal with it is obviously impossible. If immediate care is required, of course you need to go ahead with it, but make the experience as positive as possible for your dog by being gentle and providing treats and chin scratches when you can.

TESS

TRAINING

More than "doing what you ask." Training your dog is much more than teaching her to come when called or to sit for her dinner. Training, if done in a way that is fun for both of you, is an opportunity to help your dog settle into her new home, to teach her how to fit in as a polite member of the family, and to strengthen your relationship.

There isn't room in this booklet for us to describe how to train your dog to do everything you might want her to do, but what we can do is 1) summarize the most important principles of positive training, 2) illustrate how training can create a lifetime of friendship and 3) refer you to lots of great resources. Here, first, are the most important principles of humane, effective training:

Be Positive. Once you learn how to use positive reinforcement effectively (we'll call it PR), you'll be amazed at how quickly you can teach your dog new behaviors. Positive reinforcement is fast, fun and effective, and the better you get at it, the faster you and your dog will work together as a team. PR is NOT spoiling or bribing your dog; it is teaching her that certain actions result in wonderful things. The basics of PR are simple—*immediately* after your dog does something good or responds to your request, give her something that makes her happy. You'll be teaching her that it's fun to perform certain behaviors and to do what you ask, rather than using fear and intimidation, as is common in many kinds of force-based training.

PR works best if you are proactive. During the early phases of training always have treats or toys within easy reach (an easy-to-reach pocket or "bait bag" is best). You might give her a treat for going potty outside—immediately after she goes—and for turning her head toward you when you say her name. If she knows sit, ask for that and present her with a chest rub or tasty treat. Don't overwhelm her with training exercises the first day, but begin in the next few days with some key exercises to get the two of you started.

One of the keys to using PR is understanding that *she* is the one who decides what is reinforcing, whether it is tiny treats, a game of fetch or a chest rub. Pay attention to her reactions to food, petting or encouragement to play, and only use the things she clearly loves the most. A dog may love chin scratches or belly rubs, but probably doesn't care for pats on the head. Shy or anxious adult dogs who were under-socialized are especially wary of hands reaching over their heads, so a head pat is a punishment for them, not a reinforcement. This is your chance to be a canine Jane Goodall—learn to observe your dog's responses carefully, and in no time you'll learn she prefers chicken over beef (or vice versa), belly rubs over head pats and the cheap, stinky toy over the new, expensive one you just bought.

Every dog is different, and adult dogs come with lots of experiences that color what feels good or bad to them. One of us just talked with a dog walker who was hired to take a rescued racing greyhound out on walks during the day. Unfortunately, the dog was terrified of the neighborhood, and had begun to associate the dog walker with being frightened, even though she is clearly a kind and gentle person. Right now the best reinforcement for the dog is to stay close to home, and learn to associate the new person with things he wants, like cooked chicken and feeling secure.

PR is most successful if you keep it up long after you think she "knows" what to do. Most people stop reinforcing their dogs too soon, so take a tip from professional trainers and keep making her happy she did what you asked for months to come. It helps to vary what you give her (a treat? belly rub? a happy dash down the hallway?) once the behavior is established, but don't stop reinforcing her, especially if there are distractions present.

Down on Dominance. Don't get enrolled in the mythology that dogs are obedient because they respect you as the "alpha." Dominance is a concept that is often misused and misunderstood in dog training, and it will do your new dog no good to become a victim of beliefs that have no basis in fact. The term "dominance" refers to who wins in a competitive situation; it has no relationship to whether a dog comes when called, sits when asked or stops barking when told. Yes, dogs need to feel that they can count on you, but think of yourself more as a teacher/parent/camp counselor, rather than a drill sergeant or alpha pack leader. This is important for all dogs, but it is especially critical for dogs who are under-socialized, shy, anxious or unsure about whether they can trust people. If your dog has an unknown history, keep in mind that you have no idea what he might have experienced in the past. Most fearful dogs are skittish because they are genetically predisposed to being shy and are under-socialized, but some truly have been abused or treated roughly by their former owners and have learned to distrust people. The last thing you want to do with any sensitive dogs is to begin your relationship by scaring them, so concentrate on positive methods that are effective as well as benevolent.

Set Your Priorities. Remember that familiar feeling of overload when you were learning something new, and you felt like your brain was starting to smoke? That can be pretty stressful, and your dog is already stressed by having to adapt to a new environment. That's why we advocate that you set priorities and decide on a few signals that are going to be the most important for you and your dog. Setting priorities will help you to focus on a few important exercises and avoid swamping your dog's already busy brain with too much information. You'll do best if you can decide at the outset which cues you want your dog to know well and perform consistently.

Usually what is most important to people is that the dog is house trained, reasonably polite when greeting visitors, is enjoyable on leash walks and comes when called if loose in a fenced backyard. But everyone's household is different. Patricia's adopted dog Lassie, who came to the farm at eleven months of age, first needed to learn house training, to greet visitors without leaping onto their shoulders, and to deal with stress or excitement without compulsively spinning in circles. Karen's 2½ year-old rescued dog Bugsy first needed to learn to come when called so that he could go on off-leash walks, to be happy rather than scared when people visited, and to respond to his new name.

Only you know what is most important for your dog to learn, but beyond house training and being able to be left alone, we suggest beginning with teaching a dog his or her name, and to sit when asked. Soon you can work on polite leash walking, greeting visitors and the beginning stages of coming when called. That's a perfectly reasonable agenda for your next three months. (Remember that mantra about patience?)

An Ounce of Prevention . . . Of course, part of training is preventing and discouraging behavior you don't want, like jumping up on company, barking for attention or urinating on the carpet. This is where training yourself comes in handy, because a natural default behavior is to let an inappropriate behavior happen, and then punish the dog for it. Unfortunately, that is the least effective way to influence behavior.

Your first step in managing inappropriate behavior is to prevent it when you can. Don't want your new dog to chew up your shoes? Then don't leave your shoes on the bedroom floor. If your dog does manage to mutilate your new boots, don't scold the dog. Remember it's your job to ensure that your dog can't chew on inappropriate things until she has learned to unleash that energy on her own toys. A big part of success in the prevention of bad habits is the establishment of good ones, so do all you can to prevent chewing on shoes by providing appropriate chew toys, or to prevent barking at the neighbors by going outside with her to play.

Do This, Not That! When you find your dog doing something you don't want her to do (notice we did not say "if"), stop and ask yourself "What DO I want her to do?" Do you want her not to jump up on company? Then teach her what you *do* want—to either sit down when they enter or to at least keep all four paws on the floor. Want her to urinate outside rather than inside? Then prevent accidents as much as you can and reinforce her for going outside every chance you get. To think this way—proactively rather than reactively—requires training yourself, but it will save you endless amounts of time and frustration. Once you learn to ask yourself "How can I teach her to do what I *want* her to do?" rather than scolding her for doing something you *don't want* her to do, life will get a lot easier. After all, if you don't teach her, how else will she know what you want?

Learning is 24/7. Whether you are consciously "training" your dog or not, she is always learning. You can't turn her brain off just because you're too tired to ask her to sit before she jumps up on you when you come home. If you discourage your dog from getting up on the couch in the morning, but let her up at night when she makes goo goo eyes at you when you're tired, she'll learn to keep trying until you give up. However, don't let that discourage you—the good news about life being one long training session is that you can make training progress faster by integrating it into your day.

Take advantage of the fact that school is always in session by getting in the habit of having small, tasty treats in your pocket at all times. Say you've decided on a new name for your dog. Start saying it 20 times a day, and every time she turns to look at you when she hears her name, give her a treat. Do this when she is not too distracted, at different times and in different locations. Voilà, soon you'll have a dog who will know her name and respond to it. As the weeks go by, begin saying her name when she is only a little bit distracted, and gradually more so, until you have a dog who responds to you even when being teased by a squirrel. (Okay, that's bit more advanced, but no matter how far you take it, you still have to start at the beginning and gradually work up to tougher situations.)

Add in Some Tricks. Although everyone knows that dogs need physical exercise, their need for mental exercise is often overlooked. Dogs need to use their brains just like we do, and getting your new dog's brain cells buzzing is as good for you as it is for her. Not only will learning a new trick or two keep her busy (in a good way!), you can also use tricks as a way of teaching manners. Want to teach her to be polite to visitors? Teach her to "Wave" or "Go get your toy!" and practice so that she'll do it even when the doorbell has just rung and visitors are entering. Want her to get some exercise while you watch your favorite TV show? Teach her to find a hidden toy or treat that you stashed away during a commercial break, and she'll spend the next five minutes racing around trying to find it while you settle into the couch.

One of the best aspects of trick training is that people typically become light-hearted and forgiving when teaching tricks. That's a great attitude to have when you're doing any kind of training, so you might want to think about all the things you ask your dog to do as circus tricks. You can also use tricks to help with stressful situations. Patricia taught her Border Collie, Willie, to "Take a Bow" on cue, and uses it whenever he begins to look tense. Not only does the trick itself cause him to stretch and relax his body, he has learned to regulate his own emotions by doing it himself. The flip side, however, is to be careful that the trick you are teaching doesn't make the dog more nervous. For example, if your new dog is a bit anxious, don't try to teach him to lie down and roll over. That puts him in a vulnerable position, and might make him even more nervous. Instead, in that case, teach him to do something that puts his body in a more confident position, like holding his tail up on cue. Whatever tricks you choose, focus on teaching only one or two at a time to avoid overwhelming your dog.

Time to Start Training Classes? It's not a good idea to take a new dog into a training class environment until you've had a chance to get to know him. Every dog is different, so it's hard to suggest a specific time period, but it would be wise to wait at least a month or so. Classroom settings, full of unfamiliar people and a swirl of unknown dogs, can be intimidating for any dog, so wait until you've had a chance to see how your new dog behaves in new environments, around new people and when meeting unfamiliar dogs. If your dog seems nervous and uncomfortable in any of these contexts, you're much better off starting with a private session with a well-respected trainer.

If and when you are ready to go to class, be sure you take yourself to the right one. Training perspectives vary greatly, ranging from methods that include hanging a dog in the air with a choke collar for "disobedience," to classes in which you must take a pledge to be 100% positive at all times. We advise that you contact the business owner and ask to visit a class without your dog. When you do, look for no more than 10 or 12 dogs per class, a good trainer/dog ratio (perhaps one for every 5-6 dogs), a class in which barking and rowdiness is effectively but humanely kept to a minimum, and an emphasis on using positive reinforcement rather than force-based methods. Don't hesitate to ask the trainers about their background and experience, if they go to seminars (and what kind), what books they recommend, and if they are certified by any professional organizations.

Once your dog is in a class, watch him carefully for signs of anxiety. Is he continually yawning, turning his head away, agitated and unable to settle at all, or the reverse—lying stiff and motionless? Any growling or barking at other dogs? Won't take treats that he'll scarf up at home? If the class is well run, the trainers will also be watching your dog to ensure that he is a good match for the class. Don't be distressed if a trainer comes up to you on week two or three and suggests that a class might not be the best alternative for your dog. You're not "failing" or "flunking," you're being taken care of by a professional who is concerned that your dog is being harmed in a group setting, rather than benefiting from it. Every time a trainer excuses a dog from class he or she is losing money (you should receive a refund), so be clear that this is being done for your benefit. A constructive class policy is to apply class fees to a private session with a trainer or behaviorist, thus avoiding a situation that might set your dog back, while still getting the coaching you need.

The Benefits of Private Trainers. If you can, it is often a good idea to call in a private trainer after your dog has been home for a few weeks (and sooner if problems arise). Why not spend an hour with someone who works with dogs for a living, who has worked with hundreds or thousands of families and might be able to save you needless trouble in the future? In spite of assumptions to the contrary, dog training isn't always intuitive, and a consultation might be well worth the time and expense.

We provide advice to help you find a good, local trainer in the back of the booklet, but get references from your vet, other trainers and friends about experts in your area who are skilled at helping families integrate new dogs into new homes.

Slow and Steady. Did we mention the word patience? Oh, we did? Well, here we go again. (Be patient with us!) It often takes over a year to fully integrate a dog into your household. If you currently have an adult dog who is well trained, it's easy to forget how much there is for a dog to learn. Whether a dog is a puppy, an adolescent or a mature adult, learning to be an upstanding member of your personal society takes time. Remember, even though she's not a puppy, your new dog has a lot to learn. Some dogs will come with a history or a temperament that makes settling into your home even harder, but with a little patience, compassion and knowledge of humane and effective training, you'll be on the path that leads to you and your dog being buddies for years to come.

The Play's the Thing. Play is a great way to strengthen your bond, teach useful skills and exercise your dog's body as well as her brain. But just like people, dogs vary in what kind of games they like to play. Some dogs love fetch, while others, who have no interest in bringing back a soggy ball, would love to play with other dogs. Let your dog tell you how she'd like to play. Offer a few different kinds of toys, experiment to see if she'd like to run after a ball and try to engage her with a rope or a squeaky toy. See the *Resources* section for some ideas about how to use play to enhance your relationship with your dog.

I Don't Wanna Play! Not all adopted dogs are going to be playful. Some just aren't interested and may never be, while others have simply never learned how. Dogs who grow up in neglectful situations and who never had toys to play with can take a long time to learn to enjoy them. Many of these dogs will eventually play with toys, especially if they see other dogs do so, so don't feel badly if your rescue dog looks at you with blank eyes when you hold up the expensive toy you just bought. Patience (surprise, surprise) is an asset in this process because it can take a year for some dogs to start playing. Other dogs develop their play mojo quickly—sometimes even within a few days.

Toys Toys Toys. Object play is great because it is often the safest form of play, it can be used to teach manners and it allows the dog to play by himself as well as with others. Not all dogs are interested in objects, but there are ways to entice dogs to develop an interest in them. Try a variety of objects, because although there are dogs who love every kind of toy, most dogs have preferences. The basic categories of toys are balls, fleece toys, hollow rubber toys like Kongs™, squeaky toys, and ropes. Offer your dog options and perhaps you'll find that a dog with no interest in balls goes nuts over anything that squeaks.

To get dogs interested in a toy, play a little "hard to get." Play with the toy yourself, bouncing it, waving it through the air a bit, or dragging it along the floor. If the dog shows any interest, let her have the toy by tossing it in the air or showing it to her. Don't tease her by keeping the toy too long—just try to model having fun with the toy. To get a dog interested in a hollow toy such as a Kong™, fill it with something amazing such as hamburger, peanut butter, or cheese, and let the dog lick the food out. Sometimes the movement of the food-stuffed toy elicits the dog's interest, and the good feeling associated with the toy will help create an interest in objects.

Some Types of Play Can be Dangerous. We advise against rough-and-tumble wrestle play with any dogs, but especially adult dogs of unknown history who may or may not know how to play. As fun as this type of play can be, the risks of bites due to the high arousal it can cause are not worth it. Similarly, chase games can be wonderful, so while we love the game of having your dog chase you, especially as a reinforcement, we urge caution. It's easy for some dogs to turn chase games into "nip the person" games, so wait until you and your dog know each other better, and then decide whether your dog can handle this style of play.

Kids and Play. Few activities are more enjoyable than watching dogs and kids having fun as they play together. However, it's not so fun if someone gets hurt, the kids run back to the house crying or the dog becomes afraid of children. To keep everyone safe and happy, keep the following in mind: First and foremost, do not allow rough housing of any kind between the children and the dog. It's unwise for adults to engage in this sort of rough-and-tumble play, but it's even riskier for kids. Take our word for it, this kind of play can overly arouse dogs, and put children at risk of being bitten. It is also important that kids not play chase games with dogs. The risk for children getting hurt is too high when dogs chase them. As predators, even the best of dogs can get nippy if they start chasing small mammals who move fast and erratically.

Conversely, if kids chase dogs, there's the risk of either the dogs becoming frightened or of learning that it's fun to run away from people. Chasing dogs as part of a game often ruins any chance of a reliable recall and it can teach dogs to run away when you reach to take them by the collar. Finally, while we think tug is a great game for adults to play with most dogs, we do not recommend it for kids. That's another game in which dogs can become overly aroused and it's not reasonable to expect children to be able to monitor the dog's emotional state. Bottom line: It's not fair to put either dogs or children in a situation that oh-so-often leads to trouble, and it's our job as grown ups to prevent it from happening. See the *Resources* section for some great books on helping kids and dogs enjoy one another.

OFF YOU GO WITH OUR BEST WISHES!

Well, here you are, sharing your life with a new dog who arrived with a full set of experiences and expectations. Unlike puppies, adolescent and adult dogs have already learned a great deal about how to behave in the world. Some of what they've learned might be great, and will allow them to ease into your household. Others have learned to potty in the house, to be afraid of strangers or that it's fine to leap up onto the counter and eat the roast you'd planned to serve for dinner.

It takes time and knowledge to learn to live with other adults, whether they have two legs or four, so repeat the "patience" mantra on a daily basis, take it one day at a time, use the suggestions and resources noted in the rest of the booklet, and give *yourself* treats as often as you do your dog. We hope that we've helped make adopting a dog fulfilling and fun for everyone. May you all be happier than you ever dreamed.

~ ~ ~ ~ ~ ~ ~ ~ ~ ~ ~ ~

What follows is a resource for those of you who are having some behavioral challenges, whether the issue is that your dog hasn't read the chapter on house training or won't come into the living room because he is afraid of the ceiling fan. Of course, we can't provide enough information to solve all behavioral problems in this small booklet, but the next section will help you get started at turning things around.

GADGET

BEHAVIOR PROBLEMS 101

Where'd My Perfect Dog Go? Many dogs are inhibited when they first come into a new environment, especially if they've had a relatively isolated life. Over time, they'll feel more comfortable, and begin behaving like their true selves. That might mean they'll start cuddling on the couch instead of lying warily in the other room, but it also might mean they'll start growling over a piece of food dropped onto the floor. We tend to think of the amount of time it takes a dog to acclimate in threes: three days, three weeks and three months. Relatively confident, stable dogs tend to settle in around the third day (not coincidentally, it takes people about three days to settle into a new environment.) Many dogs need three weeks under their collars to begin to relax in a new home, and the more sensitive souls need a good three months. (Note: if you have rescued a dog who has suffered deprivation or ill treatment, perhaps one who grew up in a small cage and was never let out, it can take over a year for your dog to come into his own, and even then his behavior will likely be different than if he'd had a better start.)

He's Not Acting Like They Told Us He Would! It's common to be surprised by your new dog's behavior. Perhaps the foster family told you he was perfectly house trained, but now he's urinating in the back bedroom. Or maybe the shelter's behavioral evaluation revealed no signs of possessiveness around food, but suddenly Chester is growling at your children over the dinner bowl. The fact is that behavior is "context dependent," meaning that all social animals behave differently in different environments. We all know this intuitively about ourselves: Are you the same person at a tense business meeting as you are at home on Sunday morning? Are you a basically calm person who goes crazy when your favorite team wins a big game? Dogs especially often behave differently in a group setting, like a shelter or foster home with lots of dogs, than they do in a home in which they are the only dog. Evaluations in other contexts are still valuable—we strongly support objective and well-done ones—but a dog's behavior in one environment is never 100% predictive of his behavior in another. So don't waste energy fussing over how he behaved the day before you brought him home, spend it observing how he behaves now, and on what you can do to help him be his best self in the future.

Keep Track. Written journals and video recordings are useful tools to get clarity about a behavioral problem. Professionals do this with their own dogs all the time, knowing that it helps them with their own challenges, as much as it does their clients. Another benefit of even a simple, casual journal is to help you notice and appreciate your dog's progress. When something changes slowly it can be difficult to notice, and there's nothing like keeping a record to remind you how far you and your dog have come. We can't tell you how often clients have come in for a follow up appointment and actually forgotten the original reason they came to see us because it has been resolved. If the initial consultation was about helping the dog be comfortable when home alone, the next might be about barking at dogs. "But how is Jake doing when you have to leave him home alone?" we'll ask. "Oh (pause) . . . he's fine about that, but his barking at dogs who walk by is driving us crazy."

Uh Oh. What Have I Done? Don't panic if you see signs that your dog is going to be more like Marley and less like Lassie. As we said earlier, it will take weeks or months to know who you really have, just as first dates are only a start to getting to know someone you've just met. The dog who panics in a crate the first time you leave her alone may be able to handle the same situation a week later with some minor changes on your part. The dog who quietly growls when your neighbor comes to visit may have never met a man wearing a hat and parka, and eventually might end up being his best buddy.

That doesn't mean you should ignore issues that come up, or excuse them because you got your dog from a rescue and you assume he's had a difficult life. You'd be wise to pay attention to signs of problems—barking when left alone, going stiff and silent when touched, quiet growls or loud barking when visitors arrive—but don't panic about them either. If you can, contact the place or organization from which you acquired the dog. Don't worry that you are "bothering them." Honest and true, they'd rather hear from you now rather than six months down the road when the problem has become a habit and your family is ready to go on strike. This would also be a great time to contact a professional trainer or behaviorist for advice. Do yourself a favor and don't wait too long. We can tell you from experience that most people DO wait too long before seeking help, and it makes treatment more difficult. In other words, don't panic, but don't close your eyes and hope a behavior problem will go away.

In the following pages, we discuss the most common behavioral problems encountered by people who have adopted adolescent or adult dogs. We wish we could somehow magically condense full treatment plans into a small, accessible booklet, but somehow our fairy godmothers have not performed the magic to make that possible. We can, however, discuss the most common behavioral problems of adopted dogs in new homes and summarize some treatment basics. The *Resources* section lists additional sources of information if you need more help.

Take Heart. Most behavioral problems are manageable or treatable. Just about every dog, no matter what their age, comes with a need to learn new skills or change some behaviors in their new home. This often surprises people when they get an adult dog—we seem to have very different expectations of dogs once they're no longer "puppy cute," and are often less forgiving of older dogs who still need some training. But every dog needs to adapt to a new environment and a new family, so take heart if you're looking at your adopted dog right now and wondering what you've gotten yourself into. A crisis of confidence is so common that it should be considered a universal part of the adoption process. You might not have the perfect dog in two weeks, but if you are patient and persistent, you well might have a dog whose presence in your life creates joy beyond your dreams and expectations. If you are dealing with a behavioral problem, it's helpful to remember that anyone who adopts a puppy has two to three years of training in front of him. If it only takes you a year, you are well ahead of the game, right?

SEPARATION ANXIETY

Don't Go! Once they are familiar with a new home, most dogs are content to cozy up in a crate or a comfy room while you are gone, but some become anxious at just the thought of being left alone. These dogs may bark, howl, pace and drool, or chew up anything within reach while you are gone. When a dog is behaving badly because he is panicked about being left alone, we call it "separation anxiety." (We'll call it SA from now on.) Dogs from shelters have a slightly higher rate of separation anxiety, but we don't know if it's caused by being surrendered, or whether the behavior is what got them into the shelter in the first place. If you find that leaving your dog is becoming a problem, here are some things for you to consider:

Bored or Scared? The first step is to figure out why your dog is behaving problematically. Just because he chews on the pillows or urinates on the rug doesn't mean he is anxious about being left alone. Perhaps he hasn't learned yet that pillows aren't chew toys, or that good dogs only potty outside. If chewing is the only problem, then manage it by keeping temptation away while you're gone. If your dog has an occasional accident in the house then skip to the *House Training* section below and consider the fact that either your dog isn't really house trained yet, or may not be able to hold it as long as you'd like. However, chewing and urinating in the house can also be signs of separation anxiety. Here's what to look for to determine if your dog truly has separation anxiety:

• *Signs of nervousness as you get ready to leave*: Dogs who are anxious about being alone will follow you everywhere, pacing, whining, drooling and even refusing food once they clue in to the signs that you are preparing to leave the house.

• *Chewing or scratching at entrances and exits*: If your dog's destructiveness is restricted to the windowsills or the doorway, the behavior is more likely to be related to SA than simply inappropriate chewing.

• *Urinating and defecating when alone in the house:* If this never (or rarely) happens when you are home, but happens even if you are gone from the house for a brief period of time, it may be a sign of SA.

• *Repetitive barking, howling, pacing, or drooling while left alone*: We're not talking about vocalizing in response to seeing a squirrel or someone walk by the house, but about dogs who will bark or howl for hours on end. If you're not sure how your dog behaves when you're gone but you are suspicious that he doesn't settle down, use a video or tape recorder to find out. Don't think that because he's quiet when you come back home that he is quiet the rest of the time. Many dogs stop vocalizing as soon as they hear your car in the driveway, long before you have a chance to hear them barking. Neighbors can help too, especially if you ask by saying "I want to be sure that my dog and I are good neighbors. Can you help us out by letting me know if Paladin does any barking when I'm gone?"

Treatment for SA. The good news is that SA is usually responsive to treatment. The bad news is that it takes some planning and attention on your part, and can take, on average, about six weeks to turn around. If you are sure that your dog has SA, your best course of action is to consult with a behaviorist and/or thoroughly read about how to treat it. Two books we suggest are *I'll Be Home Soon!*, which Patricia wrote, and *Don't Leave Me! Step-By-Step Help For Your Dog's Separation Anxiety* by Nicole Wilde. If your dog has a mild case of anxiety about being left alone, following the suggestions below might be enough to turn things around. However, if the problem is more serious, don't hesitate to avail yourself of more resources, including consulting with your veterinarian about whether medications can help your dog during the treatment process.

• *Too late*: Never correct your dog for having had an "accident" in the house. If your dog worries about what is going to happen when you return, she'll just worry all the more about your leaving. Don't be fooled by what some people believe is a "guilty look." Studies have shown that dogs are not "guilty," but are trying to appease their owners with these postures. Punishment after the fact will not improve the dog's behavior the next time he is left alone, and if anything, will just make things worse.

• *Keep comings and goings low key*: This in itself is not going to cure SA, but it will help model that departures and arrivals are not emotionally loaded events. Try quietly saying hello to your dog when you come home, and waiting to pet or play with him until after you've settled in.

• *Take the meaning out of your "departure cues:"* Pinpoint exactly what you are doing when your dog initially becomes anxious during your departure routine. Usually it is well before you leave the house, and is an action, like getting your coat or picking up your keys, that he has learned to associate with your absence. Once you're aware of what your dog first responds to, start to help him disassociate those actions with the emotion of anxiety. If car keys are the trigger, then pick them up 25 times a day when you are *not about to leave*. For example, pick up the keys while you're going from one room to another, or sitting down to watch television. The idea is to desensitize him to an action that he presently links with feeling anxious about your impending departure.

• *Make your "departure cues" the sign that good things are coming:* You can also teach your dog that picking up your keys or walking toward the door with your coat on means that he is going to get a toy stuffed with his favorite food. The trick here is to link the beginning parts of leaving with the toy or the food so that he LOVES it when you pick up your keys. ("Wheee! She's picking up her keys!! That means I get a toy stuffed with my favorite food!! Yeah!)

• *Avoid, as much as possible, leaving your dog alone and loose in the house for long periods until he becomes accustomed to it:* For mild cases, you can try putting down a hollow toy stuffed with food and leaving the house for just a few seconds. Many dogs will be so focused on the food they will barely notice you're gone, but they'll get used to your leaving while they are feeling happy and secure. Gradually you can leave for longer and longer periods of time. If you have to leave for extended periods of time, try to either have friends come over or take the dog with you. Some dogs are fine in the car, but not the house—just be careful about the temperature outside and the danger of overheating in a vehicle. If necessary, you can leave your dog in a safe, secure place in the house where he can't do himself or your home too much harm. Make this a different place than where he is when you work on treatment. For example, leave him loose in the house with a stuffed toy for five minutes, but put him in a crate or small room if you have no choice but to leave him alone for a few hours.

• *Consider helpful products:* There are a variety of products that help dogs with SA, from DAP (dog appeasing pheromone), body wraps, homeopathic remedies and medications from your veterinarian. None of these work for all dogs, but we've had good luck with all of them on one dog or another.

TROUBLE SHOOTING FOR HOUSE TRAINING

Having Trouble? It's as true of adults dogs as it is for puppies—some are easy to house train and some are a bit more challenging, but the range of responses widens in adult dogs. Some dogs will come completely house-trained, and after three days of House Training 101 you never have to think about it again. Other dogs have been raised in neglectful circumstances, in which they had no alternative but to eliminate where they live. Needless to say, this makes house training more difficult, but not necessarily impossible. Karen fostered a spaniel who had previously spent long periods of time confined so that she could not possibly hold it until she was let out. She eliminated in her crate numerous times in the first couple of weeks at Karen's house, but after about a month, she started to get the hang of eliminating outside, and was fully house trained not long after. Patricia's Cool Hand Luke was let out only once a day in his first year of life before she got him, and it took a good six months to house train him. Once he learned the new rules, Luke was 99.99% reliable the rest of his life, so that six months of work was well worth it. If you have a dog with a difficult history, perhaps rescued from a puppy mill or a neglectful owner, find out all that you can about how the dog was raised and start right away to help him to learn how to regulate his bathroom behavior.

Good News. The good news is really good, and there is lots of it. First, the steps required to teach a dog better bathroom manners are simple and straightforward. There's no need to learn rocket science here. In addition, most dogs can be rehabilitated, even if they came to you going potty in their own beds, and the few who can never quite get it straight can be managed without too much trouble. Of course, you know there's always a cloud behind the rainbow, and the not-so-good news is that following the steps required to house train a dog older than five months can take a bit of time and energy to pull off. But the pay off is worth it, and if your dog has a problem now the chances are good that it will be but a distant memory a year from now.

House Re-Training 101. Here's how to proceed if you find that your dog has not gotten the message about where to use the restroom:

• *Rule Out Medical Issues:* Ensure that your dog is not fighting a medical problem. Have your veterinarian do a thorough exam to rule out issues that make it impossible for your dog to control her bathroom habits.

• *Think Prevention:* Do all you can to prevent accidents so that your dog doesn't develop bad habits. If he's eliminating in some areas and not others, close off the areas where he tends to go. If he tends to eliminate anywhere and any time, keep him on leash so that you can monitor his behavior more closely. Keep a journal of the time of day that the accidents occur, and take him out more frequently during those periods. Remember that just because he can sleep through the night without an accident doesn't mean he can last for as many hours when he is awake. (The same goes for us, too, right?)

• *Three Options:* At all times, Chief or Brownie should be either 1) be inside and watched by you, 2) outside with you so that you can reinforce any urinating or defecating immediately after it happens, or 3) in a small area like a crate, preferably where he sleeps and possibly eats. (We'll discuss what to do if your dog potties in his crate later on in this section.)

• *Be Prepared:* Always be ready to give your dog a tasty food treat immediately after he eliminates outside. If your dog is going inside the house, you need to pull out the good stuff for when it does happen outside. Saying "Good Dog" or giving him a little pat on the head can't begin to compete with a piece of chicken! You want your dog to think "WOW! All I did was pee on the grass and she gave me a snack. I'm going to do this more often!" Keep treats handy in your pocket or by the door to ensure that you have them when you need them.

• *Clean up Accidents:* Be sure to clean up all accidents carefully. Urine puddles especially must be treated with products specifically designed to eliminate odors. This isn't just for your sake (although that would be enough), it's also a critical part of teaching a dog to go potty outside. Dogs identify bathrooms by smell, just as we do by sight (where's the sign for the rest room?), so you need to ensure that there is no smell in the house that says BATHROOM HERE. Purchase a commercial enzymatic deodorizer made for this purpose, or if King just peed on the carpet and you have no supplies, soak as much of the liquid up as you can and treat it with white vinegar. Do not use soaps or carpet cleaners because they will tend to set the odor rather than take it away.

Didn't Read the Book on Crates? Do you have a dog who eliminates in her crate? It's actually not that uncommon. Some dogs may eliminate in their crate because they are nervous about being left alone (see the section on Separation Anxiety.) Others were forced to potty where they sleep, and have never learned how to control their own bladders. If this is the case, don't panic. Many of these dogs—often small breeds commonly abused in puppy mills—can be left alone in an ex pen (a small easily set up pen you can put up in any room) and taught to go on potty pads.

Patience. Wait, didn't we say that already? How many times now? Well, this is one of the times that you might have to bring out your most patient self. As we mentioned earlier, dogs who have been raised to eliminate in their own beds are the hardest to turn around, but we know lots and lots of success stories, and we are hopeful that your story will be one, too.

CHEWING

Boy is This Fun! Except maybe not for you, if your dog is chewing on the legs of your grandmother's four-poster bed. We all know that puppies have to learn what is an appropriate chew toy and what is not, but it's often a shock when a full-grown dog comes running out of the laundry room with your knickers in his mouth. But remember, whether young or old, your new dog doesn't know how you classify the objects in your house. Your home is new to him, so assume he knows nothing when he first arrives. That means practicing due diligence and picking up everything at mouth level that he might chew on by mistake. Your goal for the first few weeks should be to prevent inappropriate chewing and establish the habit of chewing on his chew toys, and only on his chew toys. You can do that by focusing on prevention (doors closed, remote control out of reach) and by providing a good selection of appropriate chew toys.

Adolescent Dogs Love to Chew. Prevention is especially important for adolescent dogs. Most dogs surrendered at shelters and to rescue groups are adolescents, the "free to a good home in the country" age, during which dogs often present behavioral challenges to their first owners. Destructive chewing is a common problem when dogs are eight to fourteen months old. This often comes as a surprise because once dogs are past their first puppy months they often appear to be "fully trained." However, as they grow into their teenage period they can revert back to getting into trouble. (Sound familiar to any parents out there?) We've been there—it's frustrating to think you have a problem licked and then discover that it's cropped up again a few months later. But it is very common for teenaged dogs to become obsessed with chewing, so keep that in mind if you've just brought home a dog who is believed to be younger than two or three years of age. Yup, it really takes them that long to grow up, and longer to become as emotionally mature as we'd like them to be. Seem like a long time? If it does, compare it with human development and take heart.

So what do you do if your new dog comes equipped with an overly active mouth? The answer is relatively simple (although it's true that "simple" is not a synonym for "easy!") Just pretend that you have a puppy in the house who doesn't know beans about what to chew on and what to avoid. Tidy up the house as if you had a toddler in the room, hide or coat all electric cords with a noxious taste, get rid of sugarless gum and take away any poisonous or dearly loved plants. In the meantime, bring home a sampling of chew-appropriate dog toys, paying careful attention to what your dog likes, and what holds up long enough to be worth the price. Prevention is the key here until your dog learns that he has his toys, you have yours, and you're not interested in sharing.

RESOURCE GUARDING

Uh oh. Rosie growls at you every time you reach for the chew toy . Your son tries to pet Bingo while he's eating, and Bingo has begun snapping at him. If you are experiencing this kind of behavior problem, we want to encourage you to contact a professional right away. Growls and snaps are warnings that can lead to serious injuries or to an otherwise cherished dog being returned to the shelter or rescue, so you are wise to seek professional help. In the meantime, work towards the goal of preventing escalation of the problem, and beginning the initial phases of changing your dog's responses. Talk to the whole family and get everyone on board with the following suggestions:

Prevention is Critical. As much as possible, eliminate potential sources of conflict. Write down everything you can think of that triggers a response, being mindful of subtle signs of tension like a stiff body and a closed mouth, and use that list to help you prevent problems. Don't wait for a full-blown snap to be aware she's warning you off. Feed her in her crate if that's an option, or in a closed room if she is nervous while she eats her dinner. Avoid asking her to jump up on the couch if that's where she becomes possessive when another family member tries to sit down, and encourage her to be happy in her own dog bed on the floor.

Starting right now, everyone should avoid reaching toward or touching the dog if she has anything you think she'll treasure, such as food, special toys, or even a spot on the couch. Eventually, of course, you'll work toward being able to take anything away from her, but for now, the prevention of possessive aggression is important. If she learns that growling will get you to go away, the quicker she'll be to do it next time, and the more likely the problem will escalate into something more serious.

She's Got My Cell Phone. Now What? Don't respond to her possessiveness by forcing her to defend herself. Rather, if she grabs a sock from the laundry, go get a piece of a stinky, tasty treat, wave it in the air from ten feet away and let her sniff the air. If the food is good enough, she'll drop the sock and come running. To keep her from learning to steal toys to get a treat, ask her to sit a few times before you give her the treat. That way she'll think the food is a reward for doing what you asked, not for stealing socks. If she has something she shouldn't that is valuable or could harm her, distract her away from it with food or the doorbell, and take it away when she's not looking. If it's not valuable and not going to hurt her, don't make a fuss, but think about how you can prevent the same thing from happening in the future.

If she is grouchy around her dinner bowl, and you have to walk by her while she's eating, toss pieces of food into her bowl as you walk closer, and stop tossing food as you walk away. If she's grumpy about sharing the couch, teach her to jump off on cue (for something she wants even more), and ask her to get down before you approach. Or, create a warm cozy bed for her on the floor and encourage her to sleep there rather than on the couch or the bed.

Don't Punish Growling. If you do, you might take away her warning system, so that the next time she'll skip the growl and go right to biting. You might express your disapproval with a shocked "What was that?!" but do not attempt get into a fight with your dog over an object. In some cases, you'd win, but then, in others you'd lose and either way you've just confirmed her fears: "If a person comes anywhere near me when I have a chew toy, horrible things will happen!"

Seek Help. If problematic possessiveness lasts longer than a few weeks and includes growling, snapping or biting, please enlist the help of a professional. The details of a program to *counter condition* your dog are beyond the scope of this book, so join forces with a professional and design a plan to teach her that the way to get what she wants is to be patient and polite, not by flashing her pearly whites at the family. Keep in mind that dealing with a dog with this kind of issue is never risk-free. If you have any concerns, or become afraid of what your dog might do, stop right away and get professional help.

I DON'T LIKE TO BE TOUCHED!

Growling and Snapping When Touched. No one wants to hear growls from a new dog when you try to pet him, but it is important to recognize their value. Growls and snaps are warnings—signals that dogs use to communicate that something is making them uncomfortable. That's one reason why we advise you not to discipline your dog for growling—the last thing you want to do is punish your dog for trying to communicate with you.

Please Don't Touch Me! Many dogs who have been neglected or under socialized are nervous about being touched. Some may shrink away nervously, while others will act on their fears by telling you to cut it out with a hard stare or quiet growl. Others may be in pain, and are trying to tell you to please, please stay away from an area of their body that hurts them. If you find that your dog is resistant to touch in a particular area but not any others, be sure to take your dog in for a full evaluation by your veterinarian.

If the vet is confident that the problem is not related to a medical condition, or if that condition has been treated, begin a conditioning program in which you teach the dog to associate touch with something that makes him happy. Say, for example, that your dog doesn't like it when you reach for his collar. In this case, reach only a few inches toward his neck, and give him an extra tasty treat. Repeat that 5 to 10 times in a row, teaching him that when you reach toward his collar something wonderful will happen. After a few sessions, if he is responding well, the next step is to reach toward him, lightly and briefly touch the collar, and as you do, release something yummy into his mouth with your other hand. If you can, try this two or three times a day and avoid touching him in that area otherwise. Gradually work your way to holding on to his collar for longer periods, until his behavior makes it clear that he's changed his mind from "Don't touch me!" to "Please hold my collar!" Only move to the next stage when he is happy with what you are currently doing.

The success of this program is dependent upon everyone in the household agreeing to desist from petting, hugging (especially scary!) or even reaching toward the dog except when you are actively teaching him to like it. This can be especially difficult if you have young children in the house, but even adults find it hard to resist petting dogs whenever they feel like it. It's important to do all you can to enroll the entire family in the importance of going step-by-step—perhaps you'd be wise to initiate a reinforcement program for them? ("You'll get cookies if you go the whole day without pestering the dog!") Of course, if your dog has actually bitten anyone in the household or is consistently growling or snapping, please seek professional help right away. Do NOT take any advice that says you "have to get dominance over your dog" by grabbing him by the scruff and/or throwing him to the ground. If your dog is afraid of you, he'll just become more so, and if he's simply warning you off because he is fearful, you'll just make it worse.

THE FEAR OF STRANGERS

A common Problem. Lots of dogs are nervous around unfamiliar people. Heck, lots of *people* are nervous around unfamiliar people, so we shouldn't be surprised! Even young puppies vary greatly in how they react to strangers, because "shyness" is, in part, mediated by genetics. The environment and early development also play important roles, so the responses of adolescent and adult dogs to unfamiliar people can range from hysterical joy ("OH WOW! It's a PERSON!") to cowering behind your legs or growling out threats like some hermit in a shack with a shotgun.

Men Aren't So Bad, Honest. Many people believe that their dogs have been abused by men in the past because the dogs are now afraid of men. But as we noted above, the fear of strangers can be inherited. No matter what their history, shy dogs, with very few exceptions, are more afraid of men than women. We don't know why that is true, but speculate that deeper voices, bigger jaws, bigger chests, an overall larger size, and a different way of moving through space might have something to do with it. Perhaps, given a dog's olfactory abilities, it relates to the scent associated with higher levels of testosterone. Thus, don't assume that in the past some nasty man beat your dog; it's far more likely that your dog was born a bit shy, and was not well socialized when he was younger.

The Many Faces of Fear. Keep in mind that fear can be expressed in many ways, from hiding in the closet to full-throttle barking and growling. Even dogs who bite are often doing so because they are fearful. If your dog cowers away from visitors, stands stiff and still while being petted, or growls and barks aggressively, he may very well be nervous around unfamiliar people. In mild cases this could be something that you can handle, without the help of an expert, but if there is any sign of potential aggression contact a local professional as soon as you finish reading this section. (See the *Resources* section for how to find a good trainer or behaviorist.)

Teach Your Dog to Love Visitors. We've had a lot of clients who liked that their dog was "guarding" their house by aggressively barking when visitors arrived. Take it from us, this is not a good situation. You are at more risk from a lawsuit over a bite (or even someone being frightened) than you are at being invaded by burglars. Besides, what if the "visitors" are paramedics? The fire department? This is a legitimate concern; emergency responders tell us that one of their most common problems is trying to deal with a "protective" dog while they are trying to save someone's life. Don't worry that you'll destroy any chance your dog would protect you if necessary; if your dog has it in him to protect you when you are truly in danger, he probably will. And, perhaps most importantly, it's a hard life to be fearful every time the doorbell rings, so for your dog's sake, help him be more comfortable around people he's never met.

Don't Force It. Because it is tempting to do (and so commonly done), we want to caution you to avoid forcing your dog to "love visitors" by making him stand still while people pet him. Equally problematic is requiring him to get a food treat by screwing up his courage and snatching it out of a stranger's hand. Ask your house guests to avoid petting your dog, but to let the dog come to them if he so chooses. If he is comfortable enough to receive petting, make sure it's under his chin or on the side of his face, not on top of his head.

Strangers = Chicken! Love Chicken, Love Strangers! Now that we've told you what NOT to do, here's what you should do: Teach your dog to be happy when unfamiliar people drop over by asking the visitors to toss treats on the floor when they enter the house. This keeps a comfortable distance between the visitors and the dog, and teaches the dog that good things happen when the doorbell rings. Don't force an interaction. (Warning: this is the hard part!) Ask your visitors to avoid petting the dog or to interact beyond tossing treats. It's often a good idea to teach the dog to go to a crate or back room when the doorbell rings, let the visitors enter the house and sit down, and then let the dog out to greet them. Most dogs are more comfortable once strangers (to them) have gotten past the doorway and are already seated on the couch (but be aware the dogs may be nervous once the visitors stand up again.)

If your dog is cautious of strangers, it's a good idea to help your dog be comfortable with people outside of the house as well as inside. You can use the same method that we described above. As we advised earlier, don't force an interaction by making your dog tolerate people coming up to him and petting him when he's not ready for it. Ideally, set up situations in which your friends can toss treats to your dog while remaining at a comfortable distance. If that's not possible, give treats to your dog yourself as soon as he spots an unfamiliar person. With enough repetition, many dogs will look forward to seeing people on the street because it's linked with things they love. Obviously, this can be a complicated topic, and we are unable to do it justice here, so if your dog is moderately or severely afraid of strangers, please avail yourself of other resources. See the *Resources* section for more detailed help with this problem.

No Hurry. No need to hurry here, it might take a shy dog a good year to be comfortable with people he's never met. That's okay, what's the hurry? Fear is one of our strongest emotions, and can take time to fade away, even in the best of circumstances. If you are the owner of a naturally shy or under socialized dog, it's unlikely you'll ever be able to turn him into a party animal. That's okay, what's important is to honor your dog and create a good life for him, even if it's not exactly like the life you originally envisioned.

He's Getting Worse, Not Better. Remember when we mentioned that it can take days, weeks or sometimes months before a dog's "true" nature comes out? This is especially true of fear-related behavior. It is common for extremely fearful dogs to quietly put up with visitors, being in a bit of a state of shock, until they get their paws on the ground and have enough confidence to act on their fears. Thus, the dog who stands quietly as people enter during her first month in her new home, perhaps with body stiff and mouth closed, may escalate to barking aggressively by month two or three. Long before then, as soon as you realize she's looking even a bit uncomfortable, begin conditioning her to love it when people come to call.

Don't be discouraged if your progress doesn't always go smoothly and you experience setbacks. Ups and downs are typical any time you are trying to change behavior. But don't hesitate to contact a professional if you begin to get worried that your dog's behavior is degrading, or you are becoming afraid of how he'll act when people enter the house. If you find yourself saying, "I think he'll be okay," stop right there, remind yourself that's another way of saying "I'm worried he won't be," and take action to get things turned around. You might find help in Patricia's book, *The Cautious Canine* or other books listed in the *Resource* section, but there's nothing like having a coach by your side when working through this issue if it becomes serious.

BEHAVIOR PROBLEMS BETWEEN DOGS IN THE HOUSE

You can go a long way toward preventing serious problems between your dogs by being observant of, and acting on, signs of tension between them—before things degenerate into aggressive encounters. That's why we're starting this section with a list of common signs of tension between dogs. Don't panic if you see one or two (a dog quietly growling at another dog on day one does not a crisis make), but develop a habit of observing their interactions and behavior to help you evaluate how things are going between your dogs. Common signs of tension between dogs include:

• One dog communicating threats to another through hard stares and stiff postures.

• One dog slinking around the house and clearly avoiding the other dog.

• One dog hogging resources either through hard stares, growls or bites. Those resources can be anything the dog values, including food, toys, access to sleeping areas, or the best treasure in the house—you.

• You find that you are tense and anxious about what might happen between your dogs. Listen to that inner voice, it is often right, even if you don't know why.

• Play time involving dogs who are frequently standing up like rearing horses, or whose play often degrades into increasing levels of over arousal or aggression.

It is not unusual for newly acquainted dogs to growl, snap, or show their teeth to one another during the first few days or weeks of becoming acquainted. Don't panic if your dogs are showing some of the milder signs of tension, but do continue to monitor them, being alert to any clues that tension is mounting or that new signs of trouble are appearing. If you see things escalating, we advise you to consult with a qualified behaviorist or trainer.

But The Foster Home Said He Was Great with Other Dogs! This is another behavior that is context dependent. Your new dog may have been fine in a pack of six, but not comfortable living in a home with just one other dog. Or perhaps he was polite when walking in one neighborhood, but now has targeted the sweet German Shepherd down the block on your evening walks. He may get along beautifully with females, but not do well with other males. On the other hand, he may have come with a warning tag attached: "Does not play well with others." No matter what the history, you've got what you've got, which is a dog who is not always getting along with members of his own species.

If You're Having Problems. Here are some important things to keep in mind:

• *Cancel out the Competition*: Feed dogs in separate rooms or in crates, and avoid leaving treasured toys on the floor.

• *Avoid over-arousal:* Many fights occur when dogs are highly aroused during play or periods of excitement (think about sports fans at a big game), so avoid letting dogs become excited to the point of being out-of-control. Put the dogs in another room when company comes, keep your own greetings low key, and don't "hype" the dogs up with your voice or your actions during play sessions.

• *Give each dog down time:* Social interactions can be as tiring for dogs as they are for people, so be sure to give each dog time by himself. This is especially important for older dogs who are clearly not up the to energy levels of a younger, more energetic newcomer.

• *They all want you!:* Go out of your way to spend one-on-one time with each of your dogs, even if you have a herd of them and it's only five minutes of special attention. If your resident dog(s) learns that the newcomer means he's lost what he wants most—you—it will be hard for him not to resent the new kid on the block.

• *Don't put fuel on the fire:* If you see your dogs threatening each other, be careful that your own energy doesn't end up adding to the tension. If your dogs are standing still and growling at each other, take a breath and in a low, relaxed voice, ask them to sit, or clap your hands and say "Want to go on a walk?" Avoid using a loud, angry voice, or a shrill, frightened one, and do what you can to break up the tension. Don't rush toward the dogs to grab their collars unless you have no choice—this can create a fight rather than prevent one.

• *If there is a fight:* First try distracting the dogs with a loud noise, but if that doesn't work, don't start yelling at the dogs to stop. That often makes fights worse. The next safest way to stop a dog fight is to use a flat object, like a board, to separate them, but you might not have one stored in your living room. If there are two adults in the house, each one can grab a dog by the base of the tail and pull the dogs apart. Grabbing a dog by the collar is the most natural way to respond, but it also puts you at greater risk of being bitten. Regrettably, interfering in a dog fight always puts you at some risk. If your dogs have had a fight, call in someone to advise you of where to go from here.

Good Things Come to Those Who Wait. Begin a program in which each dog learns that she gets what she wants by being patient and polite. Teach the dogs to sit and stay in a group, and release them one by one by saying their name in a lilting voice (rather than saying "okay" which releases them all). Teach a possessive dog that he can get petting from you, and maybe even a treat, if he sits and waits while you pet the other dog. If one dog pushes in between you and another, move the offender back by quietly "body blocking" him backwards, and ask him to sit and stay while you pet the other dog. Then release Mr. Pushy Boy and give him a good pet too. Message: Good things come to those who wait.

Don't "Support the Alpha." Some sources still repeat that old story about deciding who is "Alpha" and always supporting that dog—letting that dog go through doors first, eat first, and even supporting that one in a dog fight. This approach just reinforces bullies, and we strongly advise you not to follow such a program. We've seen too many dogs badly injured when owners tried to reinforce a "pack leader," so throw that concept away and work towards teaching your dogs that "Patient and Polite" is the name of the game.

Reach out for Resources. We wish more than we can say that this booklet could provide you with a magic formula to solve any and all behavior problems between household dogs. However, social relationships are complicated (as anyone with parents, a spouse, friends or children knows!) and don't always lend themselves to quick fixes. One written resource that some have found helpful is our booklet *Feeling Outnumbered?*, but don't hesitate to call in the experts if you think one of your dogs might be injured or you're concerned about at least one dog's quality of life.

REACTIVITY TO UNFAMILIAR DOGS

As with behavior problems between dogs in your home, reactions to unfamiliar dogs can also be a complicated situation. If your new dog appears uncomfortable when he sees other dogs in the neighborhood, there are several things you can do right away:

• *Don't Force Interactions*: Don't let other dogs greet yours with the hope that it will be "okay." Better safe than sorry. Just turn and walk the other way or cross the street if a dog is approaching you before you've had a chance to get to know how your new dog will respond.

• *Go With What You Know:* Let your new dog meet a known quantity before he meets dogs you've never met yourself. Ask someone you know with a friendly, well-socialized dog to come over and meet your new one. If you can do this with a few dogs, one at a time, you'll get a better sense of how your dog behaves around unfamiliar dogs without putting him at risk of being frightened or in a dog fight.

• *Prevention is Your Friend*: If your dog is beginning to react problematically, barking and lunging at dogs on the street for example, don't feel guilty about avoiding those situations. Rather do all you can to prevent outbursts of barking and lunging. Think of them as bad habits, like having a cigarette when you're trying to quit. Take walks at quiet times and give him exercise in the yard or the house while you work on a treatment plan. Always be ready to turn and go the other way when you see another dog if you think it will get too close for comfort. Response prevention is a powerful part of treatment, so don't feel like you are "cheating" by avoiding a bad situation until you get the problem turned around.

• *Avoid Group Classes*: Don't take a dog who is reactive to other dogs to a regular training class in hopes he will magically improve. In many cases, he'll get worse. You are much better off scheduling a one-on-one session with a trainer, or getting into a reactive dog class if there is a good one in your area.

• *Get Help:* There are many ways you can help a dog who is nervous around unfamiliar dogs. We can't do them justice here, but we can refer you to some helpful resources. Avail yourself of books, DVDs (listed in the *Resources* section), one-on-one coaches and "Feisty Fido" classes. You may never end up with a dog who is comfortable at the dog park, but almost all dogs can be conditioned to walk comfortably and politely on leash around other dogs.

FEARFUL DOGS: LIFE CAN BE SCARY

Don't Make Me Go Up the Stairs! Adolescent and adult dogs come with a full set of luggage that carries both their genetics and their early experiences. Those factors can combine to create a dog who happily blunders into everything and anything with an exuberant joie de vivre or a shy, neglected dog who is afraid of her own shadow. Dogs who have been raised outside might be afraid of light fixtures, stairs, uncarpeted flooring, the television, and the beeping noise from appliances. Some dogs are extremely sound sensitive and are frightened by unfamiliar noises. This is another trait that is influenced both by genetics and experience.

Other dogs are afraid of unfamiliar shapes, or the movement of a ceiling fan. While you see your home as a haven of love and safety—perhaps you rescued your dog from abusive conditions—your new dog might perceive it as a house of horrors, simply because everything is so unfamiliar. How you respond to those fears will make a significant difference in how fast your dog settles in and becomes comfortable in a new household. Some dogs, in spite of your best efforts, may never relax in some contexts, but there is a lot you can do to help your dog relax in a new environment.

I'm Telling You I'm Scared! First and foremost, you can help her by being able to read subtle signs of fear. Just because these expressions and postures are subtle to us, doesn't mean a dog isn't truly frightened. We suspect that if we could ask dogs, they'd say they are often visually screaming to us that they are scared, and what's wrong with us that we can't "hear" them? Beyond the obvious signs of fear—trembling, running away, whining and yelping, body crouched and tail tucked, dogs have many ways of expressing fear. Here are some of the more subtle signs that your dog is experiencing fear or anxiety:

- Yawning when she's not sleepy.
- "Tongue flicking" such that her tongue darts quickly out from the front of her mouth, rather than from the side of her mouth as if she were anticipating food.
- Consistently turning her head away from something, or hiding behind you.
- Refusing to take high quality treats that she normally loves.
- Showing rounded eyes with large pupils.
- Sweating from her paws or panting when it's not that hot.
- "Busily" sniffing the ground, as if to avoid something else.

Desensitizing and Counter Classical Conditioning. Most dogs will become comfortable with "scary" things over time, but you can help alleviate her fears by learning how to use desensitizing (we'll call it DS) and counter classical conditioning (CCC). When desensitizing a dog, you repeatedly expose the dog to "low intensity" versions of the frightening object or event. If the scary thing is the sound of the vacuum cleaner, you'd turn it on 25 times a day, but just for one second at a time and only when your dog is as far away as she can get, perhaps in another room. If your dog is afraid of a ceiling fan, you'd turn it on repeatedly through the day, but just for a second. Gradually you'd increase the intensity of the exposure, assuming that your dog responded well to the previous phases of DS.

We've found that adding in CCC can do a lot to help a dog become comfortable with something new and scary. CCC is a process in which your dog learns to link something she loves with the thing that used to scare her, such that she begins to feel good whenever either are presented. For example, to begin a CCC program for a dog afraid of a ceiling fan, you'd turn it on for one second as you would in DS, but then you'd immediately give her a treat and turn off the fan. That way she learns that the fan means a tasty yummy is coming, and she'll grow to love the sound of the fan as much as she loves the taste of the treat. Remember how you felt about the loud, jarring bell that signified recess in school? Didn't you grow to love it? That's a good example of CCC (assuming you liked recess, that is), and illustrates the power of this very useful method.

It won't work however, if you go too far too fast. If seeing a ceiling fan for even one second scares her so much she won't eat a treat, then you are at risk of teaching her to associate feeling fearful with the treat—the reverse of what you want! In that case, begin when she is in another room and slowly work your way up to getting her closer and closer.

Warmer, Colder. You can also use a process called "shaping" to teach her to do something she seems afraid of, like going up the stairs or entering a new crate.

In this form of operant conditioning, you reinforce her for doing any part of the behavior you'd like her to perform. If she's afraid of the stairs, you could give her a treat for walking to the base of them, then for sniffing the first step, then for putting just one paw onto the first step, perhaps over a series of sessions.

Clicker training, in which you use a hand-held clicker to help her know what behavior will lead to a treat, is especially useful for this type of training. Clicker training can be a wonderful way to help fearful dogs learn that they have some say in their environment ("If I do X, I can make that wonderful noise happen, and then I'll get a treat!") and to begin to build some confidence. A cautionary note: Some sound sensitive dogs are afraid of the sound of the clicker. You can get around that problem by using the clicker in your pocket or held behind you, or by using one of the softer clickers designed for such dogs. Or, you can replace the use of a clicker with a different marker, such as saying, "click" or "yes." The *Resources* section has some options to help you get started with a clicker.

Put it On Cue. One useful way to help dogs who are fearful is to help them prepare for something that makes them nervous. For many dogs, the worst part is being taken by surprise, so if you can alert them to the fact that something's coming, they do much better. In the case of a dog who is scared of the fan, you'd say "Here comes the fan!" right before you turn it on and give her a treat. Or, you could have a generic "What's that?" that you use whenever you spot something that you think will make her nervous. If you follow the phrase with a treat, eventually she'll learn that "What's that?" means there's something new in the environment to look at, and boy is she glad, because it means she'll get bacon! However, be careful that you don't teach the reverse of what you want. If she starts to look nervous when you say "What's that!" you're going backwards, so observe carefully to ensure that this is a helpful rather than a harmful method.

Slow and Steady Wins the Race. Here we go again, but patience is going to be your best friend when dealing with fear-related problems. It can take dogs many months, and sometimes a year or more, to become comfortable in a new environment if they have a combination of genetically-mediated shyness and have also had a difficult time as a growing puppy. Don't panic if in the first weeks your dog acts fearfully around things inside or outside your house. If she barks and backs away from a garbage can in the street, understand that she has no idea what it is. For all she knows it's a monster about to consume you both. If she's already scared, let her back up a bit, and then say "What's that?" and give her a treat right after she looks at it.

I'm Terrified of Everything. Sadly, some dogs will come to you with such a horrible history that they arrive psychologically damaged. Dogs who were kept in tiny, squalid cages for years as breeding dogs in puppy mills are simply not capable of handling environmental change without it being traumatic. If you have a dog who is extremely frightened of everything, including you, it's important to understand that most "normal" advice about welcoming a dog into your home will not be especially helpful. If your dog is afraid of simply everything, your first step is to provide her with a safe place, usually a crate in a quite area. If at all possible these dogs should be placed in a home with another dog, whose presence is often comforting and who can act as a model later on as you try to bring the frightened one out of her shell.

These kinds of dogs deserve their own booklet, and we can't go into an entire treatment plan in this one, but here are some basics that will be helpful if you have been so kind as to rescue one of these poor, abused souls:

• Provide a safe place like a crate in a quiet area and let the dog stay there, except for potty breaks, for weeks if necessary.

• Keep a collar on the dog, and if it's possible to do safely, a short leash dangling so that you don't have to pick the dog up to move her around.

• Talk to your veterinarian about the appropriateness of anti-anxiety medications if the case is severe.

• Use adjunctive therapy, including DAP or other brands of "dog appeasing pheromones," aromatherapy, homeopathic preparations or Chinese herbs to help calm your dog.

• Let the dog watch you toss treats to another dog, so that she can observe a member of her own species interact freely and happily with a human.

• Expect that the dog will not be house trained, and that she has learned to potty where she sleeps. Deal with this at first logistically, by putting easily washed bedding in her crate and keeping her on surfaces that can be cleaned and de-odorized easily.

• Most important, understand that your little dog may never be comfortable in some settings, and that it takes years for some of these dogs to completely relax.

It's important to be realistic here—these are not easy dogs to adopt, and everyone who does so should be aware of what they are getting into. That said, what a generous and wonderful thing for a family to do! If this section describes your dog, our hats are off to you. Just turn the word "patience" into a daily mantra and give up any thoughts that somehow you are failing if you don't "fix" this dog in a few months. Remember, someone else permanently damaged your little dog—you are just picking up the pieces as best you can, and offering an innocent dog her first chance for a decent life.

Sometimes Love is Not Enough: We would love to tell you that every dog can flourish in every home, but the truth is that, no matter what you do, sometimes a dog and family are not a good fit. This is not a failure on your part, it is an acknowledgement that you have learned what your dog needs, and that you are dedicated to helping him find it. If you have tried and tried and find yourself continually stressed and worried, or if no matter what you do, your dog is not happy, it is a kindness to consider finding him another home. If you are in this situation you'd be wise to consult with friends, your veterinarian, trainer or behaviorist, and objectively ask what your dog needs, what your family needs, and whether another home would be best for everyone involved.

~ ~ ~ ~ ~ ~ ~ ~ ~ ~ ~ ~ ~ ~

Whatever your dog's problems, be they big or small, we wish you all the luck in the world, and hope that in the years to come you'll look back on any troubles you're having now as ancient history—interesting, but long ago and far away!

PIPIT

ACKNOWLEDGEMENTS

It takes a village to write a book like this, and we are more grateful than we can say to all of those who have contributed their thoughts, ideas and feedback on earlier versions. Specifically, we'd like to thank Jim Billings, Meg Boscov, Margaret DeSmet, Khris Erickson, Lisa Lemberger, Katie Martz, Aimee Moore, Denise Swedlund, and Chelse Wagner for putting their time and energy into the booklet.

We are also grateful to Julie Mueller and Jennifer Weitzman at Jam Graphics, and everyone at the printing company Suttle-Straus, for generously donating a portion of their typesetting and design fees out of the pure goodness of their hearts in support of the adoption of homeless dogs everywhere. You can learn more about them at http://www.jamgd.com and www.suttle-straus.com. They are also responsible for turning our messy word document into a real live book, and designing covers for all our booklets.

Thank you to the hundreds of people who responded to our request to send us photos of their own rescued dogs. There were so many photographs we wish we could have used! The "winning" photographs are on the cover and at the beginning of each section. You can read about each of the dogs at www. patriciamcconnell.com. Thank you to Shannon Baade, Sarah Babcock, Sarah Baker-Jones, Allison Duncan, Megan Kime, Lauren Mack Cooper, Min McGregor, Eliza Nardone, Robin Reed, Tammy Wallace, Kimberly Wang, and Wendy Wilson for sending in such great photographs, and allowing us to use them in the booklet.

RESOURCES

GENERAL TRAINING

Dunbar, I. 1996. *How to Teach a New Dog Old Tricks*. Berkeley, CA: James & Kenneth Publishers.

King, T. 2004. *Parenting Your Dog*. Neptune, NJ: TFH Publications.

McConnell, P. and Moore, A. 2006. *Family Friendly Dog Training: A Six-Week Program for You and Your Dog*. Black Earth, WI: McConnell Publishing.

Miller, P. 2007. *Positive Perspectives 2: Know Your Dog, Train Your Dog*. Wenatchee, WA: Dogwise Publishing.

Pryor, K. 2005. *Getting Started: Clicker Training For Dogs*. Waltham, MA: Sunshine Books

Reid, P. 1996. *Excel-erated Learning: Explaining in plain English how dogs learn and how best to teach them*. Berkeley, CA: James & Kenneth Publishers.

Sdao, K. 2006. *Know Way, No How? – The Science and Art of Clicker Training*. Seminar DVD Set, 2nd Edition.. Eagle, ID: Tawzer Dog Videos.

Yin, S. 2004. *How to Behave So Your Dog Behaves*. Neptune, NJ: TFH Publications.

UNDERSTANDING DOGS

Aloff, B. 2005. *Canine Body Language: A Photographic Guide*. Wenatchee, WA: Dogwise Publishing.

Bradshaw, J. 2011. *Dog Sense: How the New Science of Dog Behavior Can Make You a Better Friend to Your Pet*. New York, NY: Basic Books.

Clothier, S. 2005. *Bones Would Rain from the Sky: Deepening Our Relationships with Dogs*. New York, NY: Warner Books.

Handelman, B. 2008. *Canine Behavior: A Photo Illustrated Handbook*. Wenatchee, WA: Dogwise Publishing.

Hetts, S., Estep, D. and Grant, D. 2000. *Canine Behavior: Observing and Interpreting Canine Body Postures* DVD. Denton, TX: Animal Care Training, Inc.

Hetts, S. and Estep, D. 2003. *What Dogs Need and How They Think*. Littleton, CO: Animal Behavior Associates.

McConnell, P. 2002. *The Other End of the Leash: Why We Do What We Do Around Dogs*. New York, NY: Ballantine Books.

McConnell, P. 2005. *For the Love of a Dog: Understanding Emotion in You and Your Best Friend*. New York, NY: Ballantine Books.

ADOPTING DOGS

Benjamin, C. 1988. *Second-Hand Dog: How To Turn Yours Into a First-Rate Pet*. New York, NY: Howell Book House.

Miller, P. 2010. *Do Over Dogs: Give Your Dog A Second Chance For A First Class Life*. Wenatchee, WA: Dogwise Publishing.

Shaughness, C. & Slawecki, C. *Puppy Mill Dogs Speak!* Charleston, SC.

BARKING

Estep, D. and Hetts, S. 2006. *HELP! I'm Barking and I Can't be Quiet*. Littleton, CO: Animal Behavior Associates.

Ryan, T. 1998. *The Toolbox for Remodeling Your Problem Dog*. New York, NY: Howell Book House.

CHILDREN AND DOGS

Pelar, C. 2007. *Living With Kids and Dogs. . .Without Losing Your Mind.* Wenatchee, WA: Dogwise Publishing.

Shumanfang, B. 2006. *Happy Kids, Happy Dogs: Building a Friendship Right from the Start.* Raleigh, NC: Lulu Enterprises.

Silvani, P. and Eckhardt, L. 2005. *Raising Puppies and Kids Together: A Guide For Parents.* Neptune, NJ: TFH Publications.

CRATE TRAINING

Anderson, T. 2005. *Quick and Easy Crate Training.* Neptune, NJ: T.F.H.

McConnell, P. & Scidmore, B. 2010. *The Puppy Primer.* Black Earth, WI: McConnell Publishing.

Miller, P. 2007. *Positive Perspectives 2: Know Your Dog, Train Your Dog.* Wenatchee, WA: Dogwise Publishing.

DOG-DOG REACTIVITY

London, K. & McConnell, P. 2008. *Feeling Outnumbered? How to Manage and Enjoy Your Multi-Dog Household, 2nd Ed.* Black Earth, WI: McConnell Publishing.

McConnell, P. and London, K. 2009. *Feisty Fido: Help For the Leash Reactive Dog, 2nd Ed.* Black Earth, WI: McConnell Publishing.

McConnell, P. 2010. *Treating Dog-Dog Reactivity.* Seminar DVD. Eagle, ID: Tawzer Dog Videos.

McDevitt, L. 2007. *Control Unleashed—Creating a Focused and Confident Dog.* South Hadley, MA: Clean Run Productions.

Sdao, K. 2006. *Cujo Meets Pavlov! Classical Conditioning for On-Leash Aggression*, Seminar DVD. Eagle, ID: Tawzer Dog Videos.

Stewart, G. 2010. *Organic Socialization DVD – BAT for Aggression and Fear in Dogs*. Eagle, ID: Tawzer Dog Videos.

FEARFUL DOGS

Jacobs, D. 2008. *A Guide to Living With & Training a Fearful Dog*. Guilford, VT: Corner Dog Press.

McConnell, P. 2005. *The Cautious Canine: How to Help Dogs Conquer Their Fears, 2nd Ed*. Black Earth, WI: McConnell Publishing.

Wilde, N. 2006. *Help for Your Fearful Dog: A Step-by-Step Guide to Helping Your Dog Conquer His Fears*. Santa Clarita, CA: Phantom Publishing.

HOUSE TRAINING

Dunbar, I. 2004. *Before and After Getting Your Puppy: The Positive Approach to Raising a Happy, Healthy, and Well-Behaved Dog*. Novato, CA: New World Library.

King, T. 2004. *Parenting Your Dog*. Neptune City, NJ: TFH Publishing

London, K. and McConnell, P. 2003. *Way to Go! How to Housetrain a Dog of Any Age*. Black Earth, WI: McConnell Publishing.

McConnell, P. & Scidmore, B. 2010. *The Puppy Primer*. Black Earth, WI: McConnell Publishing.

Miller, P. 2008. *The Power of Positive Dog Training*. New York, NY: Howell Book House.

PLAY

Bennett, R. 2007. *Off-Leash Dog Play: A Complete Guide to Safety and Fun.* Woodbridge, VA: Dream Dog Productions.

London, K. and McConnell, P. 2008: *Play Together, Stay Together: Happy and Healthy Play Between People and Dogs.* Black Earth, WI. McConnell Publishing.

Miller, P. 2008. *Play With Your Dog.* Wenatchee, WA: Dogwise Publishing.

Silvani, P. 2007. *Playtime: Win, Lose, or Draw.* DVD. Eagle, ID: Tawzer Dog Videos.

RESOURCE GUARDING

Donaldson, J. 2002. *Mine! A Practical Guide to Resource Guarding in Dogs.* Wenatchee, WA: Dogwise Publishing.

SEPARATION ANXIETY

McConnell, P. 2000. *I'll Be Home Soon! How to Prevent and Treat Separation Anxiety.* Black Earth, WI: McConnell Publishing.

Wilde, N. 2010. *Don't Leave Me! Step-By-Step Help For Your Dog's Separation Anxiety.* Santa Clarita, CA: Phantom Publishing.

FINDING A TRAINER OR BEHAVIOR CONSULTANT

Training methods vary greatly, and anyone can put up a shingle as a "dog trainer" or "canine behaviorist." We suggest first asking friends, boarding kennels and veterinarians for references, and then doing your own screening by interviewing the person you would work with before they meet your dog. Ask them what kind of training they have had (seminars attended? books read? apprenticeships?) and what kind of methods they use. Ask if they have credentials of any kind (CAAB? CPDT?) Look for trainers or behaviorists who understand how to effectively use positive reinforcement, rather than just giving it lip service. You might ask them to describe, for example, how they would handle a specific situation, like a dog growling at you over the dinner bowl. The best people will have a thorough knowledge of positive reinforcement, classical and operant conditioning, as well as experience working with a variety of breeds.

It is equally important to find someone that you are comfortable with—if an internal voice tells you that something isn't right, don't hesitate to say thank you and walk away. If you possibly can, observe your potential helper and coach working with other people and other dogs. If that's not possible, meet the trainer first to talk before he or she starts to work with your dog, and be sure that they are specific and clear to you about how they plan to do so. We don't want to scare you off, there are lots of amazing trainers out there, but there are also those who still subscribe to the "show 'em who's boss!" theory of training and those who love dogs but have no additional qualifications. Take it from us, your dog may feel secure within the benevolent boundaries of your home, but the last thing an adopted dog needs is to be coerced and threatened as part of "training." Training should be something that you and your dog can't get enough of, like practicing a sport that you both love, so find someone who can help you create smiles and wagging tails, rather than a list of ways to dominate and intimidate your dog.

USEFUL WEBSITES

http://abrionline.org

> A website that is dedicated to improving the quality of life and relationships for animals and people, filled with advice and training tips from experts around the United States.

http://animalbehaviorassociates.com

> Suzanne Hetts, Ph.D. and Dan Estep, Ph.D. are both Certified Applied Animal Behaviorists whose website provides practical and science-based information to help you understand and change your dog's behavior.

http://www.apdt.com

> The Association of Pet Dog Trainers (APDT) is a professional organization of individual trainers who are committed to becoming better trainers through education.

http://www.thebark.com

> The website of Bark magazine (also called the "New Yorker of Dog Magazines, and the magazine whose phrase "Dog Is My Copilot" is seen everwhere) where you can find articles, art and discussion about all things dog. Karen is a regular blogger on this site.

http://www.dogstardaily.com

> Ian Dunbar and Kelly Gorman Dunbar's website about training and behavior, featuring articles, video and blogs by experts from around the United States.

http://www.dogwise.com

> The biggest online store for buying dog books and DVDs. Karen's husband (jokingly) begs her to let him hide the credit card when he sees her at this site.

http://fearfuldogs.com/

An excellent resource for fearful, shy, or anxious dogs.

http://www.theotherendoftheleash.com

Patricia's blog site, a forum for people who are both intellectually and emotionally fascinated by the behavior of the animals at both ends of the leash.

http://www.patriciamcconnell.com

Patricia's site listing her training tips, books, DVDs, speaking schedule and Blog Posts.

http://positively.com

The official website of trainer and television personality Victoria Stillwell. Victoria uses positive methods and does a great job of seeing the world from the dog's point of view.

http://www.speakingforspot.com

Nancy Kay, DVM, is a veterinarian and dog lover known for providing information about how to be a medical advocate for your dog.

OTHER BOOKS BY THESE AUTHORS

Way to Go!
   How to Housetrain a Dog of Any Age

Feisty Fido
   Help for the Leash-Reactive Dog

Feeling Outnumbered?
   How to Manage and Enjoy Your Multi-dog Household

Play Together, Stay Together
   Happy and Healthy Play Between People and Dogs

OTHER BOOKS BY PATRICIA McCONNELL

The Other End of the Leash
   Why We Do What We Do Around Dogs

For the Love of a Dog
   Understanding Emotion in You and Your Best Friend

Tales of Two Species:
   Essays on Loving and Living with Dogs

Family Friendly Dog Training (With Aimee Moore)
   A Six-Week Program for You and Your Dog

Puppy Primer (With Brenda Scidmore)

How to be Leader of the Pack and have your dog love you for it!

The Cautious Canine:
   How to Help Dogs Conquer Their Fears

I'll Be Home Soon!
   How to Prevent and Treat Separation Anxiety

The Fastidious Feline
   How to Prevent and Treat Litter Box Problems

All books, booklets (and many DVDs) are available
at www.patriciamcconnell.com

See Patricia's blog at www.theotherendoftheleash.com
and Karen's blog entries at www.dogbehaviorblog.com
and
www.thebark.com/content/karen-b-london-phd-0.

Patricia B. McConnell, Ph.D. is an Ethologist and Certified Applied Animal Behaviorist who has consulted with cat and dog lovers for over 23 years. She combines a thorough understanding of the science of behavior with years of practical, applied experience. Her nationally syndicated radio show, *Calling All Pets*, played in over 115 cities for 14 years. She is the behavior columnist for the *The Bark* magazine and Adjunct Professor in Zoology at the University of Wisconsin-Madison, teaching "The Biology and Philosophy of Human/Animal Relationships." Dr. McConnell is a much sought after speaker and seminar presenter, speaking to training organizations, veterinary conferences, academic meetings and animal shelters around the world about dog and cat behavior, and on science-based and humane solutions to serious behavioral problems. She is the author of thirteen books on training and behavioral problems, as well as the critically acclaimed books *The Other End of the Leash: Why We Do What We Do Around Dogs* and *For the Love of a Dog: Understanding Emotion in You and Your Best Friend*.

Karen B. London, Ph.D. is an Ethologist, Certified Applied Animal Behaviorist and Certified Pet Dog Trainer, who has focused on evaluating and treating serious behavioral problems in dogs for 12 years. She is an Adjunct Professor in the Department of Biological Sciences at Northern Arizona University, teaching a tropical field biology course in Nicaragua. Dr. London's research and scholarly publications address interactions between species that live together, defensive and aggressive behavior, evolution of social behavior, communication within and between species, learning, and parental investment. She is the training columnist for *The Bark* magazine, a blogger for thebark.com and dogbehaviorblog.com, and writes the Arizona Daily Sun's animal column, *The London Zoo*. She is on the Animal Behavior Society's Board of Professional Certification and has spoken widely about canine behavior and training in educational seminars and speeches for trainers, veterinary and shelter staff, and the public. This is her fifth book on training and behavioral issues in dogs.